Never Pay
the First Bill

Never Pay the First Bill

AND OTHER WAYS TO FIGHT
THE HEALTH CARE SYSTEM AND WIN

MARSHALL ALLEN

PORTFOLIO / PENGUIN

PORTFOLIO / PENGUIN
An imprint of Penguin Random House LLC
penguinrandomhouse.com

Most Portfolio books are available at a discount when purchased in quantity for sales promotions or corporate use. Special editions, which include personalized covers, excerpts, and corporate imprints, can be created when purchased in large quantities. For more information, please call (212) 572-2232 or email specialmarkets@penguinrandomhouse.com. Your local bookstore can also assist with discounted bulk purchases using the Penguin Random House corporate Business-to-Business program. For assistance in locating a participating retailer, email B2B@penguinrandomhouse.com.

Grateful acknowledgment is made for permission to reprint the following:
Excerpt on page 219 courtesy of Jeffrey Fox, Los Angeles
Sample letter on page 228 by Lisa Berry Blackstock/Soul Sherpa

Library of Congress Cataloging-in-Publication Data

Names: Allen, Marshall, author.
Title: Never pay the first bill: and other ways to fight the
health care system and win / Marshall Allen.
Description: 1st [edition]. | New York: Portfolio/Penguin, [2021] |
Includes bibliographical references and index.
Identifiers: LCCN 2021005233 (print) | LCCN 2021005234 (ebook) |
ISBN 9780593190005 (hardcover) | ISBN 9780593190012 (ebook)
Subjects: LCSH: Medical errors—United States. | Medical care,
Cost of—United States. | Medical care—Quality control—United States. |
Health insurance—United States.
Classification: LCC R729.8 .A55 2021 (print) |
LCC R729.8 (ebook) | DDC 610.28/9—dc23
LC record available at https://lccn.loc.gov/2021005233
LC ebook record available at https://lccn.loc.gov/2021005234

Printed in the United States of America
1st Printing

Book design by Tanya Maiboroda

To anyone who's been pushed around by
the American health care system

Contents

PART III

Employer Section

Introduction:
My Mom and Dad's Health Care Battle

’VE BEEN AN INVESTIGATIVE REPORTER covering health care since 2006, and I've been continually astonished by the unfair nature of the American medical system. It's outrageous that we pay far more for health care than the citizens of any other country without getting our money's worth. It's alarming the way big players—drug companies, hospitals, insurance companies, and others—profit by exploiting our sickness and violating our trust. I talk every day to people who are getting taken advantage of by the system.

I wrote this book to arm individuals and employers with the knowledge, tactics, and inspiration they need to stand up for themselves and the people they care about. I also wanted to counter the idea that this is always a losing battle. Lots of people are fighting back and winning—saving hundreds or thousands of dollars by the savvy way they engage the system. I wanted to empower others to stick up for themselves and save big money. Little did I know that I would need to put my own advice into practice before I was through writing. But it happened, and I want to tell you that story here because it illustrates a lot of the principles that come into play.

My two brothers and I watch over our dear parents as they age. My mom and dad agreed to let me share our family's story because they care about accountability and justice and helping others. My dad, who just turned eighty, suffers from a slowly advancing form of dementia but is in excellent physical health. After years of his decline and my mom's own health challenges, it became clear that she needed help caring for him. In the fall of 2019, at the same time I started writing this book, we made the difficult decision to admit Dad into an assisted living facility.

As a journalist, I've written almost every type of health care horror story, including those about the problems in long-term care homes. We did an extensive check to make sure we avoided any truly dangerous places for Dad. My parents and my older brother live in northern Colorado, and thankfully we found a nice assisted living facility near them. The place was expensive—more than $6,000 a month—but brand new and well appointed, with flat screen televisions, comfy couch areas, and good food. The staff was also kind and truly seemed to care about my dad.

The problem is, they got something extremely confused during the admission. My mom has my dad's power of attorney, so she has the legal right to determine what type of care he should receive. She told the staff that she would continue to pick up Dad to take him to his established primary care doctor. My older brother was with her when she signed the admission paperwork, and they both say Mom's direction was clear: Dad should not receive routine medical care at the assisted living facility. The facility's executive director still had my mom sign a consent form for the primary care group that provided medical services at the facility. Mom's understanding was that she signed it in case Dad needed emergency care, not for anything routine.

My mom and brother visited my dad almost every day or picked him up and brought him to church or family events. After he had been there for more than a month, they noticed a dramatic mental decline. He went from a warm, personable demeanor to acting lethargic and detached, almost robotic. Mom noticed but chalked it up to the dementia. Perhaps he was having a hard time with the transition.

Just before Christmas Mom got a pharmacy statement in the mail. It showed that, unbeknownst to her, my dad had been on a drug called tamsulosin, also known as Flomax, for more than a month. The statement said a nurse practitioner whom Mom had never heard of put Dad on the medication. Mom didn't understand—how could there be a new drug that she hadn't approved or known about? And who was this nurse practitioner? She quickly realized that the drug could have caused Dad's recent decline. And when she looked up the possible side effects, they aligned with his symptoms of cognitive impairment. She called the administrator at the assisted living facility and ordered them to stop the Flomax immediately. They complied. Thankfully, Dad bounced back as soon as they stopped the drug. He had recovered, but it was despite the people who were supposed to be caring for him, not because of them.

Mom had already been unimpressed by the facility. The place felt empty, they often canceled activities, and Dad didn't get enough stimulation. She had already planned on moving him out, but this sealed it. Soon after the new year he moved to a different facility, where things went much more smoothly. About two months later, we all got hit with the COVID-19 pandemic. We moved Dad back in with Mom and they have been doing great. They are so happy and content to be together.

But it turns out the medication error was only one of the problems. Soon after the move out of the first facility, the billing department from the primary care medical group came calling. They didn't have Dad's Medicare insurance information. That's because they were never intended to provide his care. But they wanted his Medicare details so they could bill for a routine exam that the same nurse practitioner had performed on Dad. What!? This was the first my mom had heard of any exam! There wasn't supposed to be any routine treatment on Dad. The bill came to $445, they said, which sounded steep to me for an exam on a healthy dementia patient.

I marveled at the irony of this situation. At the same time my dad suffered a medication error and my mom got billed for an unnecessary exam that violated her power of attorney, I happened to be writing this book about how patients can stand up for themselves when they're getting pushed around. The primary care group had stuck the parents of the author of *Never Pay the First Bill* with a bogus medical bill. Well—here we go. Game on. I had learned so many things while writing this book and now I would get to put them into practice. I knew I had the knowledge to handle the situation—it's right here in these pages. And I also had the motivation. Mom made me the point person and I began the process of unraveling the problems. I had to find out how the medication error had occurred. And I needed to persuade them to waive the bill.

Mom had already complained to the primary care group about the medication error. She said she wanted a full explanation for what had happened, and an apology. The primary care group responded with a short letter to say they were looking into it, but they seemed to miss the point. "We apologize for this medication occurrence," the letter said. That's a strange apology because they didn't call the *occurrence* what it was: an error. My dad should have never been put on Flomax.

The letter came from the nurse practitioner, so I called her. To her credit, she spoke to me and was extremely apologetic and concerned about the error. She told me that the letter should not have minimized it. "It is an error," she said. "He was not supposed to be on the medication and he did receive it."

I appreciated that she admitted it. And I could tell she was sincere. That's more than many patients ever get. She also apologized and said she was trying to figure out how it had happened. It turns out a refill request had somehow been originated at a long-term care pharmacy used by the primary care group, which has medical providers throughout Colorado. She didn't know how that had happened but assured me that she had changed her practice. She would never again approve a medication refill without checking the patient's records.

I've spoken directly to hundreds of victims of medical errors. Most of them did not get an apology when they or their loved one suffered from a medical error. Medical professionals tend to go with the language used in the letter—calling an error an occurrence, or an "incident," to avoid taking responsibility. No one ever did tell us how the pharmacy made the mistake.

Now I had to sort out what led to the bill for $445. I called the primary care group and got connected to a woman in the billing department. She explained to me that the same nurse practitioner who had made the medication error also had done an examination just days after my dad was admitted. I tried to explain that there should have been no exam at all, because my mom, who has the power of attorney, hadn't given consent. The woman from the billing department didn't want to hear about that. She just wanted Dad's Medicare insurance information so she could submit the claim.

What type of care did you provide to my dad? I asked. "Kind of like an exam," the woman said. "We're unable to bill any insurance. So we're just sitting here with a $445 balance. If he had coverage, I need to know."

What type of exam? I asked, leaning forward in my seat and taking notes on my computer. "What code did you use to bill it?"

"We used an evaluation and management—E&M—code," she said, "99328."

"What does that code mean?" I asked. "Is it based on the time spent on the exam?" I was fishing to see if they were upcoding—using a code that overstated the complexity of what actually occurred so they would get paid more. My dad is healthy as can be, except for his dementia. He had had a full exam by his primary care doctor before being admitted to the assisted living facility and was in great shape.

"It's based on level of service," the woman explained. "That 99328 would qualify as a level 5 new patient service. A little more intensive than the initial level."

A little more intensive? Basic exams are coded from level 1 to 5. Level 1 is the least intensive. Level 5 is not something a physically healthy guy like my dad would need. I later looked up the code online and saw it describes an examination that requires seventy-five minutes or more with a patient and his family, usually because the patient has developed a significant problem that requires medical decision making of high complexity.[1] I suspect that type of exam didn't happen with my dad.

The woman from the billing department was getting frustrated. If I didn't provide the Medicare insurance information, she said she would bill my mom. I asked her to please send me the medical records that justified the level 5 billing code. But I never heard from her again, and a few weeks later my mom got a bill in the mail for $445.

The primary care group had escalated the situation. Our dispute had entered a new phase. The bill caused a lot of stress for my mom. She didn't like someone coming after her for money. I knew what to do, because I had just been working on the chapters in this book about how to dispute an unfair medical bill and how to sue your medical provider if you get billed unfairly. I was excited to use these methods myself.

I talked to the director of business administration for the primary care group. We traded some phone calls and email—it took a lot of urging—but finally he sent me the medical records from the examination. He also sent the consent form that my mom had signed and claimed it justified the exam. It seemed that the assisted living facility had botched the consent process during my dad's admission, and that led to a miscommunication. The primary care group mistakenly believed it should be providing care to my dad.

But that doesn't justify leaving my mom out of the picture. The nurse practitioner should have involved my mom in every aspect of the care. There should have been no history and physical of my dad, given his cognitive limitations, without the presence of my mom, who until that point had been his full-time caregiver. The bill "needs to be waived and the account needs to be cleared," I wrote to him in one email. "Obviously you should not be billing patients for exams that are unnecessary, incomplete, and violate the patient's power of attorney."

I also called the assisted living administrator and told her what I thought had happened, and that the primary care group was coming after my mom for $445. She suggested they should waive the bill. I told her I agreed and that perhaps she could urge them to back off and let things go.

I also made it clear to all three of them—the facility, the primary care group, and the nurse practitioner—that if we didn't get the situation resolved in a way that was fair and that answered all our questions, I would escalate my concerns. I told them I would have no choice but to file complaints against the licensing boards for the nurse practitioner, the facility, and the pharmacy. Then the state regulators could investigate whether they violated Mom's power of attorney, and they could also figure out how the medication error occurred.

I think it was my brother's visit to the assisted living facility to make copies of the medical records that finally loosened them up. I live in New Jersey, so he had to make copies of all the records so we could see what consent documents my mom had signed. I also wanted to see if they had Dad's primary care doctor properly listed anywhere in the records. Sure enough, the name of his actual primary care doctor was right there on the face sheet of his medical record. The primary care group should not have been involved in any routine care without my mom's consent.

Ultimately, I was gathering these records and taking notes in all these conversations to prepare for what might need to come at the end of the line. I was prepping to sue them in small claims court—an inexpensive venue for resolving disputes that doesn't require an attorney. I have a chapter in this book about how you can use small claims court to win your health care billing battles. I was building my case, putting the evidence together, piecing together the puzzle to figure out what went wrong and who was responsible. I made it clear to all of them that we were not going to stop and were not going to back down until we were treated with the fairness we deserved.

I will give the assisted living administrator credit for being open. She welcomed my brother's visit and let him make copies of the records at their machine. They didn't charge him like some medical facilities do, which is ridiculous because every patient has a legal right to a copy of their medical records. As my brother made copies of the records, he said he sensed it might be making the administrator a bit nervous. She hovered near him and made halting conversation. "Are you trying to shut us down?" she asked him at one point.

He assured her that we had no interest in shutting them down and that we don't care about money. "We care about what's right and just for people," my brother explained.

Then he asked her if she knew what I did for a living. Yes, the administrator said, she knew I was a journalist. "You should read some of his stories," my brother said.

I sort of wish he hadn't said that because it might have tainted my case study. I try to go through these situations without people knowing I'm an investigative reporter because it allows me to get a purer picture of how the public is treated.

I don't know if my brother's mentioning my muckraking credentials did it or not, but I got a call a day or so later from the business director of the primary care group. "I'd like to see if we could come to a conclusion on this," he said. This time his tone was deferential. He said he'd spoken to the assisted living facility administrator the day before and decided we could argue back and forth forever, but that they would go ahead and clear the bill. "It's just the prudent thing to do," he said.

I didn't argue with him or talk back. One of the fundamental rules of negotiating says to keep your mouth shut if things are going in your favor. I thanked him and asked him to please send me confirmation in writing by the end of the day. He did so, and I forwarded it to my mom, and she rejoiced.

Case closed.

I didn't even need to file a case in small claims court, which bummed me out just a little.

I asked both the assisted living administrator and the primary care group business director to comment about the situation for this book, but they declined.

I was pleased to see how well the tactics I describe in this book worked for me. Some people might not blink at a $445 bill—they'd just pay it. But many Americans barely have that much in their savings account.[2, 3] My family could have paid the bill, but it would not have been right and there would have been zero accountability for everyone who made the error and sent the bill. Plus, it didn't take us more than a couple of hours total to fight the bill. Saving $445 for my mom and dad was a nice return on our investment.

It felt good to stand up for what's right and save hundreds of dollars. Now I want you to enjoy that same satisfaction and relish a similar financial reward. This book is for anyone who has ever felt bullied by the health care system. You may be someone who has a sense that you're not getting a fair shake as you see more and more money get taken out of your paycheck for insurance premiums. Perhaps you were hit hard by the COVID-19 pandemic and lost the insurance coverage you had through your job. Or maybe you are covered through a health care sharing organization, or have a high-deductible health plan, so you pay a lot out of pocket and need to make sure you get the best deal. Maybe you're younger, at the start of your career, and perplexed by our convoluted health care system. This book is going to teach you life skills that could save you hundreds or thousands of dollars every time you buy a medication, or go to the doctor or hospital, or get a lab test or an MRI.

This book will reveal the hidden tricks the health care industry uses to make your money disappear. It will also show you how to identify errors in your medical bills and what to do about them. And it will lay out the tactics insiders use to fight back. Applying these tips could save you big money, and you will also bask in the pride of standing up for yourself—and that's priceless. American medicine can be a bully, counting on us to remain passive and keep paying. I'm going to show you how to stick up for yourself and make the bully back off.

My goal is to empower you as you think about this problem.

The health care industry has conditioned us to think there's nothing we can do about the ridiculous prices and unfair medical bills. The health care industry has been making us think that it sets all the rules and our role is to passively comply. It's set us up to be victims. But it doesn't have to be this way. We can be victorious.

This book shows how to avoid unnecessary care, how to identify price gouging and fraud, and how to negotiate a bill to get it reduced. As I mentioned, I also explain how to use small claims court to sue a hospital or doctor if they aren't willing to treat you fairly. I will provide step by step instructions on how to do all those things and more.

If we don't stand up for ourselves the abuse will never stop. Our costs will continue to rise. Our coverage will get worse. Our paychecks will be even more depleted. More people will go into debt. More of us will be sent to collections. On the flip side, if we deploy the strategies in this book, we can come out on top. We won't win every fight. But if we don't try we will lose every time.

This book also has a section for employers, who have been watching the cost of the health benefits they provide climb so high it's eating into their revenue and the money they devote to paying their employees. Depending on the size of their organizations, employers could save tens or hundreds of thousands or millions of dollars while improving the health care benefits enjoyed by their workers. Nobody else is going to fix this problem for us. Let's fix it for ourselves.

I want to make sure one thing is crystal clear: No matter what you're told, it doesn't have to be this way. The American health care industry could provide better care for less money. But that hasn't been its goal.[4] And that's where we come to my reason for writing this book. I have an audacious proposal: We should be paying less for health care and getting more for our money.

My goal is to leave you feeling inspired and equipped to

overcome this problem. Please do me a favor: Contact me when you have a victory, big or small, via my website, marshallallen.com. I want to write up and share as many of your stories as I can. We can all be an inspiration to one another. And we can also share the tips and tricks and tactics that we used to win. Let's build the momentum so this movement grows, so we can finally get what we deserve: better health care that costs less.

PART I

Fighting Back

1

The Five Hidden Reasons
You Should Fight Back

I F YOU'RE READING THIS BOOK, you might have a sneaking suspicion that the health care system has been taking advantage of you. Working Americans have their health care costs rise every year, and it's been going on for decades. You may be spending a large portion of your income on insurance premiums and deductibles and out-of-pocket costs. You may have switched to a health care sharing or high-deductible plan to try to save money. Or maybe you are uninsured, or even in debt because of medical bills. If you're an employer, you've probably seen your organization's health care costs rise. It's cutting into your profit and what you can afford to pay your employees. You are not alone.

We are in a dire situation. The average premiums for a family's health insurance are greater than a typical family's house payment.[1] Many Americans have such exorbitant deductibles—the amount they must pay out of pocket before their insurance plan kicks in—that they pay cash for all but the most expensive care. Tens of millions of Americans have medical debt in collections. And tens of millions are uninsured or underinsured—numbers that spiked due to the job losses caused by the coronavirus pandemic.[2]

The health care industry has made things plenty confusing for us when it comes to getting a fair deal. We've been made to think we need someone else to figure it out, and that it's too complicated for us to handle. The industry wants us to stay lazy and keep handing over our cash without asking any questions. The industry wants us to think there's nothing we can do.

BUT THE TRUTH IS YOU CAN FIGHT BACK AND WIN.

With the right tactics and persistence you can push back and come out on top. You can stand up to the bullies in the health care system. Each battle will have varying circumstances and stakes, but similar strategies and principles apply.

But before we get to tactics, let's get to mindset. What did I learn when I fought back for my parents in the incident I described in the introduction? Here's my first observation: It can be hard to push back. It may be time consuming and inconvenient. It took me and my brother a few hours to make phone calls, gather records, email, and negotiate to understand what happened and defend ourselves from the unfair medical bill. I looped my sister-in-law into the conversation, because she's a nurse who has worked for years as a nursing home administrator. It may take specialized knowledge and it requires motivation. And even then it is still a logistical challenge. If you're reading this book, I am guessing you know this, too. But there's also a payoff for the inconvenience. It feels good to stand up for yourself and save a lot of money.

I also learned that it may be socially awkward to challenge the same people who were once my dad's caregivers. The assisted living administrator was a kind woman who genuinely cared for my family. And I had to point out where things went wrong with the care provided to my dad. That's no fun. I also had to deal with the subtle social pressure from the primary care group. They acted like my mom had done something wrong. They seemed entitled. Everyone acted like it was just routine to violate a patient's power of attorney and do an unnecessary exam and bill Medicare for it. They barely took responsibility for the medication error. They were unaccustomed to the family member of a patient asking them questions or expecting them to justify themselves. Maybe you can relate. But it's often going to be uncomfortable to tell someone to stop taking advantage of you. We should expect some pushback when we stand up for ourselves.

I learned that this process is especially difficult for a patient or caregiver. My mom felt betrayed by the way these caregiving companies did business. Her anxiety spiked when she got the bills for the exam. When she got the second bill notice she was starting to crack: "I am feeling extremely vulnerable," she wrote to me in one email. My mom already has a hard time sleeping and this stressed her out.

In addition to knowledge, you need to have grit and determination. You must have the will to fight or you will not fight at all. Many people will see the tactics laid out in this book and think: "Oh no, is it really that hard?" My wife is a peacemaker, so some of the stuff I'm writing about in this book goes against her nature. I know she would do it if you pushed her hard enough, but it would be tougher for her than it is for me and others like me. You may have to dig deep to find the motivation to go into battle.

Like the hero of any good story, you face external challenges when you fight the health care industry. Your external challenges might be your medical bills, expensive insurance premiums, medical debt, rising drug prices, and more. But like all great heroes you will also have internal challenges, the stuff in your head that will make you want to give up. You may feel like you can never understand the bureaucratic maze of our health care system. You might feel defeated when you think of understanding your medical bills. Or maybe you feel exhausted or terrified by the idea of asking your doctor or employer or hospital tough questions.

This chapter equips you to overcome the internal challenges that come with this fight. I hope the following five insights about how the health care system operates will inspire you to take on the battle. This is not the propaganda you hear in your employer's annual enrollment meeting or that you see on advertisements by health insurance companies. Those are the messages the health care system uses to perpetuate its abuse. This is the real scoop about the way the health care system works. Understanding and appreciating these five reasons you should fight back will fuel your inner drive to engage in the battle and emerge victorious.

REASON 1: We are the ones paying for health care.

I've heard people say their employer, or their insurance company, or the government pays for their health care. But we need to stop acting like someone else is funding this system. Every dollar comes from each one of us.

Let's start with the common assumption that our employers are the ones paying for our health care coverage. Let's say your boss takes you out to dinner at a five-star restaurant. You sit down to white linen, gleaming silverware, and servers who look like fashion models. It's the kind of place that gets written about in magazines. Your eyes light up when your boss tells you that your company is paying for your meal. Order whatever you want.

You don't even look at the prices. You're loving it. Sumptuous appetizers. Drinks. An entrée and, of course, one of those flambé desserts. At the end of the meal the server brings a supple leather folder to the table and sets it in front of your employer. Wow, even the check is posh. But then, to your dismay, your boss grabs your wallet, removes your credit card, and uses it to pay the bill.

You feel the blood drain from your face. You can't believe it. But it's your boss, so what are you going to say? The next day at the office it gets even worse. The boss brags to everyone that the company took you out to the fancy dinner.

You would never stand for someone taking your money and spending it on something, and then claiming they were the ones who paid. But something similar happens if you get your health care benefits through your employer.

Before the COVID-19 crisis, about 157 million Americans received their health benefits through their employer. When we accepted our jobs, we were given a compensation package that, we hope, included benefits. Employers offer wages—our take-home pay—and other benefits, like health coverage, paid time off, time off for sickness, and perhaps a retirement contribution. The benefits vary depending on the employer and the job, but they make up each employee's total compensation package. So—the employer funds the compensation package, but the compensation belongs to the employee.

Typically, employers who sponsor health benefits claim they pay for a portion of the monthly premium—often the majority. Then they say the remainder is the employee portion of the cost. It would be more accurate to say our employers are funding our health benefits via the money they have given to us as compensation. But it's our employee compensation paying 100 percent of the tab.

So, is providing health benefits an act of generosity on the part of employers? Is it an expense for them? Of course! We hope employers will be charitable with their compensation. Employers certainly shoulder the burden of compensating their employees. But they and seemingly everyone else involved in the medical industry tend to talk about paying for health benefits without acknowledging that every dollar is coming from the employee's compensation.

Here's a big reason this is important: Your wages are not rising like they should, because of ridiculous health care costs. The compensation employers dedicate for our health benefits comes from the same pool of money they would use to increase our wages. Health care costs that rise every year put them in a difficult spot. They could dip further into the company's resources to cover the increase, and often they do. Or they could raise your premiums, reduce your coverage, or make you pay more out of pocket. That's typical. Deductibles—the amount you pay out of pocket before your insurance plan pays for anything—have been rising so high that many workers are effectively uninsured. They often pay thousands of dollars out of pocket before their coverage kicks in.

Why does this matter to you? Rising health care costs consume employee compensation, and that means you get paid less. "The increasing cost of health care has resulted in relatively flat real wages for 30 years," researchers wrote in the *Journal of the American Medical Association*.[3] This trend has been going on for decades. If we don't fight back it's just going to get worse.

Health insurance companies and the government don't pay for our health care, either.

Health insurers are middlemen. Their job is to predict how much coverage will cost, then set premiums to fund it—adding about 20 percent for their administration and profit. If they're right, they make money. If they're wrong, they lose money. But no worries if they lose because they're playing the long game. They cover losses by raising rates the following year. There's no magic money tree that is funding the health insurers. They just take that money from you and me—via our employers and our paychecks, or directly from us if we're on an individual plan.

The government doesn't fund its own health plans, either. The public—people like you and me—funds the plans through taxes. Medicare, the federal government's insurance for the disabled and people over age sixty-five, is funded by taking money from your paycheck. Medicaid—the state-based program that provides coverage for low-income Americans—is also funded by our taxes.[4] Same with the Veterans Administration and every health plan for public employees, like teachers and cops. Taxpayers and workers fund them all.

Why does this matter to you? When you are grounded in the fact that this is your money, you are empowered to exercise your right to say how your money should be spent. The health care industry and maybe even our employers would like us to play along with the façade and remain passive. It might be inconvenient and uncomfortable for them if we speak up. But if we don't take a stand, then nothing will change and the industry will continue to empty our bank accounts.

REASON 2: The customer is always right, but health care power players don't consider you their most important customer.

For more than a century, the idea that "the customer is always right" has been part of the American mindset. Customers are the ones paying for goods and services. Keeping them happy is good for them and good for business.

Naturally, patients and employers assume they are the customers when it comes to getting medical care. We are the ones undergoing the treatment, after all. And we pay for it, too. The problem is, the health care industry doesn't treat us like the customers.

As I have shown, we are the ones funding health care. But think about how the industry talks about who pays for its services. The "payer," according to health care lingo, is the insurance company or government insurance plan. But calling an insurer or government health plan the "payer" is like calling your accountant the "payer" of your taxes.⁵ These "payers" take money from workers and employers and taxpayers and distribute it to medical providers. We fund the whole enterprise, but because of the middlemen we've lost our customer status.

The health care industry players instead bestow special "customer" status on one another. The insurance companies set their rates in secret with hospitals and then demand that we pay them, even if they are unfair. The insurers and drug companies partner to boost one another's profits. The brokers advising our employers don't press for a better deal because the insurance companies and vendors pay them big bonuses and commissions. The big players negotiate with one another for a bigger cut of our money, so they can earn larger returns and reward their executives with massive salaries. The industry operates like a cartel—a coalition of players working together to keep prices high and limit competition. They work together to maximize their payout because they're playing with someone else's money—ours.

Why does this matter to you? The loss of customer status helps explain why you can't get straight answers when you have legitimate questions. You get stuck on hold and sent on the robo-message runaround when you call customer service because they don't value you enough to easily resolve your problem. It would be great if we could get the price of a medical service or procedure before we undergo treatment. But the industry typically refuses to provide it. When bills are inaccurate it takes a massive effort to get them corrected. We sometimes have a hard time getting insurers to approve care that's a part of our policies. If patients have the unfortunate experience of suffering a medical error, they may get shunned by doctors and hospitals when they ask for even the most basic information.

For employers, the loss of customer status makes it hard to get detailed information about where the money they allocate to employee benefits is going, which makes it difficult to monitor costs. I've talked to employers who self-fund their plans, and they can't get carriers to stop blatant cases of fraud. The carriers are loyal to the medical providers because they want to keep their networks intact.

It's frustrating when we don't get the respect we are due as customers. But realizing the industry players operate to enrich themselves at our expense helps us to know how to position ourselves to hack the system. We need to be strategic and use different tactics to fight back because we know they won't easily acquiesce when we ask them to be fair with us. We'll need to be persistent and calculating.

REASON 3: The business of medicine exploits your sickness for profit.

A doctor can tell you to strip naked and put on a paper gown and within minutes you're chafed in all the wrong places and feeling the breeze on your hindquarters. A nurse might ask about your sexual behavior, or your use of illegal drugs, or how often you urinate. That's not exactly cocktail party conversation, but you would probably tell the truth. That's because we trust doctors and nurses.

But here's where we tend to go wrong. We trust the doctors and nurses so much that we don't realize the business side of the health industry is not looking out for our interests. Not knowing this can make us feel guilty when we push back.

Health care companies know this and exploit it. UnitedHealthcare, the country's largest health insurer, has a warm slogan: "Health plans that care for you and your family." As if it's all about you and your needs, not what's best for the behemoth's investors.

"People taking care of people," says HCA Healthcare, one of the nation's largest operators of hospitals and surgery centers. The drug giant Pfizer says its purpose is "breakthroughs that change patients' lives." The whole industry promotes itself as if it only exists for the betterment of humankind.

But by now we have decades of evidence that shows the industry is putting itself first. Its behavior doesn't align with its catchphrases. We need to separate our opinion of the industry from our affinity for the doctors and nurses and other clinicians whom we see face-to-face.

Recently a friend at my church had an unwelcome discovery. She developed an infection in the spot on her abdomen where her surgeon had performed a procedure years ago. The wound had healed but something was going wrong. It got so painful and oozy that she had to go to the emergency room, where they removed a golf ball–sized chunk of what appeared to be gauze from the wound. Thankfully, they were able to remove the "retained foreign object"—to use the industry's term for it—and they treated the infection. But then they sent her thousands of dollars in medical bills, as if she should be the one to pay for the mistake of her surgeon or whoever on the team left the surgical residue in her side.

Her insurance plan paid its portion of the bill and she and her husband paid an additional $1,000 out of pocket. They knew this wasn't fair but didn't want to get sent to collections. She also needed an additional operation to further correct the harm done by the mistake—and the hospital billed them again. Sadly, this is the standard way the health care system treats patients, even victims of medical errors. My friends are still fighting the bills, and say they feel angry that no one has taken responsibility for the error. Patients feel a deep sense of betrayal when they realize the health care business is not looking out for them.

The business side of the health care industry is masking its true priorities. It says patient care comes first but operates deceptive schemes to take our money. The business side of medicine exploits the work of front-line clinicians to reap huge profits—with little regard for what's reasonable or what patients can afford. It even exploits the clinicians themselves, causing them what some call "moral injury" and burning them out by making the focus money instead of patient care.

The profiteering schemes are only beginning to get exposed. The auditor for the State of Ohio made a massive breakthrough by examining the state Medicaid plan's pharmacy benefit managers (PBM), which manages the drugs that go to low-income patients in the state. Yeah, it takes an actual audit to figure out the fees because they don't disclose them as you would expect if they were going to be fair. Medicaid plans nationwide are in these types of cloaked agreements. The Ohio auditor found the PBMs were taking hidden fees of 31 percent to dole out generic drugs. The fees cost taxpayers $208 million in a single year.[6] To put that fee into perspective, that's like a grocery cashier charging you an extra dollar to ring up a $3 bag of chips. Our employer sponsored health plans are in similar agreements.

The cost of insulin has been rising so fast it's become totally unaffordable to many diabetics, requiring them to go without or ration it. A Senate Finance Committee investigation looked at a hundred thousand pages of internal drug industry documents and found insulin manufacturers aggressively raised prices in lockstep with one another without any significant improvement in the drugs.[7]

How about outrageous hospital prices? At the beginning of 2021 hospitals were required by the federal government to post prices for common procedures and services on their websites, including cash prices and the negotiated prices they had with each insurance company. Not all of them are complying, but many are, and it's quite a revelation. Leon Wisniewski, a data analyst and actuary who lives near Philadelphia, has been gathering the pricing information from hospitals across the country. He is working to make the prices easy to look up through his business, Health Cost Labs. He's finding astounding differences between what the same insurance plan pays for the same service at nearby hospitals and between what different plans will pay for the same service at the same hospital.

For example, Vassar Brothers Medical Center in Poughkeepsie, New York, reported that Empire BlueCross BlueShield pays an average negotiated payment of $102,381 for a noncervical spinal fusion.[8] But Northern Dutchess Hospital, about twenty-four miles to the north, reports that the same BlueCross plan pays it an average of $49,188 for the same type of spinal fusion.[9] Meanwhile, Vassar Brothers reports getting paid about $30,000 for the same procedure by the federal government through its Medicare plan. Even crazier, both hospitals are part of the same chain.

I contacted the hospital chain and they declined to comment. A spokeswoman for Empire told me, "the prices have to be taken in full context to be meaningful." She also said the prices are competitive compared with other payers. But the problem here is that Empire's prices aren't even competitive with itself!

Similar unexplained and unjustified price variation is rampant in American health care, and it's only starting to be exposed. Wisniewski called what he's finding "Exhibit A" of the hidden pricing schemes that are standard in American health care. "It's the middleman economy," he said. "It's information blocking to extract wealth from America."

Again, why does this matter to you? The business of American health care has not been dealing with us in good faith. If we keep trusting industry players who use deception to take more money from us than they should, without pushing back, we're being suckers. Be skeptical if the industry mainstays say they want to provide better value to Americans or reduce the high cost of health care. Look at what they do—and then resolve to fight back to get a fair deal.

REASON 4: The health care industry wastes obscene amounts of your money.

Policy wonks love to talk about all the health care dollars we're spending. They should focus on all the health care dollars we're wasting.

We spend about twice as much per person on health care in the United States as what's spent in most other wealthy countries.[10] And studies show we are not rewarded with better health because of it.[11] The real scandal is that there is no justification for the high cost.

In 2012 the National Academy of Medicine estimated the U.S. health care system squandered $765 billion a year—more than the entire budget of the Defense Department.[12] The academy flagged many causes, including overtreatment, excess administrative costs, and high prices. Those problems have not been fixed. More recent estimates have identified similar culprits and have come to the same bleak conclusions. A 2019 report in the *Journal of the American Medical Association* looked at fifty-four unique peer-reviewed studies.[13] It pegged the total cost of the waste at between $760 billion and $935 billion a year. One study found that simplifying the way we finance health care in the United States could save more than $350 billion a year.[14] That's more than enough to pay the health insurance premiums for every uninsured American.

A few hundred billion here, close to a trillion there, and pretty soon you're talking about real money. Added up over the years, it's costing us trillions. Remember, it's all of us—employers, workers, and taxpayers—who fund every dollar that goes into the health care system. Dave Chase, whom I feature in chapter nine, likes to call this wasted spending a tax by Wall Street on the American Dream.

The industry isn't motivated to reduce the waste. The more money it can take, the more it makes. People's employment in health care depends on our shelling out more money, whether or not it's necessary. So even though wasted health care spending is a known crisis there are few meaningful efforts to make the industry more efficient.

The waste takes a variety of forms—exorbitant prices, bloated salaries and administration, inefficient middlemen, fraud, unnecessary treatment, and more. Sometimes the wasted spending is presented as something good, like costly employee wellness programs. The vendors and wellness consultants say their programs work, but studies show the $8 billion industry is not saving money or improving health outcomes in a significant way.[15]

Knowing that so much of our money is wasted adds moral force to our demand for a better deal. It's immoral for the health care system to take your money, squander it, and then demand more. You wouldn't let anyone else treat you this way. You wouldn't run your own household or business this way, either. When the Puritans settled in the United States they brought a "waste not, want not" moral ethic that has been passed down through generations. We are a wasteful country, no doubt, but we still tell our kids to eat all the food on their plates. We all know that it's wrong to waste.

The health care industry could provide all the care you need at a lower price. But it has chosen not to, so it can keep taking more of your money. When a doctor or drug company or hospital or insurance company tells you to pay more, you know they could get by with less. Let's challenge the way they blow our money.

REASON 5: Our health care system is not broken. It was made this way.[16]

The medical industry and politicians love to present complicated and incremental proposals to reduce health care spending, as if this was one of their big priorities. But they never get anywhere close to bringing us in line with the spending of other developed countries. We need to stop being naïve. These are some of the most wealthy and powerful individuals and corporations in the world. They can pull whatever strings necessary to accomplish their goals. They have demonstrated that it is not their intent to reduce what we spend. In fact, their investors are counting on us to continue paying more. It's not an accident that we have the most expensive health care system in the world. And if the politicians—from both major parties—and health care power players wanted us to have a health care system that's equitable and fair they would make it happen. Let's face it: Reducing what you spend has not been their goal.

A couple of years ago, I got a letter from my insurance company saying that my monthly premiums were going to rise in the coming year by about 10 percent. . . . Again! I'd seen similar health insurance premium increases in previous years—10 percent one year, 12 percent another year; I'm guessing you know what I mean.

It made me wonder: Just how much more have I been paying over the years? Looking back revealed the dramatic increase in the money the health care industry has been sucking out of my paychecks.

Back in 2012, I had $199 taken out of every paycheck to cover the health insurance premium for my family. That added up to $4,776 for the year. By 2020 my employer was taking $325 out of each paycheck—and it had been even higher in previous years. So that's $7,800. Some years it was higher, but overall, in nine years it went up 63 percent. We all realize our costs are going to rise. That's just how inflation works. But from 2012 to 2020 my health insurance premiums spiked at more than five times the rate of inflation. Adding it up, I've paid more than $16,000 more for my premiums than I would have paid if they had risen at the rate of inflation. In addition, I had benefits reduced, so I ended up paying even more out of pocket. Meanwhile, I'm facing college costs for three kids and driving a minivan with more than 250,000 miles on it. My family could really use the $16,000 that's been quietly siphoned away by the health care system.

Statistics show that most people reading this book are in a similar situation. I encourage you to make this same calculation with your health care costs. It really hits home how the increase weighs us down over time. And if you're a younger person who is just entering the workforce you should be especially outraged. You're getting saddled with this inexcusable burden of health care costs when your earning power is the lowest. It's a fundamental inequity passed on by your elders.

Why does this matter to you? It's unsettling to realize the policy makers and industry insiders are not going to help you, but it's also empowering. You can fight, and you can win. Employers and working Americans can take on this challenge and bring about change—it's already happening, as I will lay out in the following chapters.

If you don't stand up to a bully, he is going to keep taking your lunch money. But if you put him in his place he might do what you want. If you're looking for motivation, remember the five reasons I covered in this chapter:

1. **We are the ones paying for health care,** not your employer, an insurance company, or the government. If you won't protect your money, they're going to keep taking more of it.
2. **The customer is always right, but health care power players don't consider you their most important customer.** Even though you are the one paying for your health care and undergoing the treatment, the industry players are teaming up to enrich themselves.
3. **The business of medicine exploits your sickness for profit.** It's life and death for you. It's dollars and cents for them. And the system is not operating in good faith.
4. **The health care industry wastes obscene amounts of your money.** The solution isn't to keep taking more money from you. The solution is to reduce the waste so you pay less.
5. **Our health care system is not broken. It was made this way.** Our elected officials and health care companies have had decades to reduce health care costs. If they wanted to fix the problem, they could. We must stop being naïve and realize that saving our money is not their intent. So we need to stick up for ourselves and demand that the system change. If we don't, the exploitation of our sickness will never stop.

I know this book is taking on what many people say is an intractable problem. I know people feel helpless. I've felt helpless, too. But the following chapters will show you how to hack the health care system so you can pay less and get more in return. I am going to reveal the playbook so you and your family can save hundreds or even thousands of dollars when you interact with the medical system. It will take some moxie and street smarts. But when you apply the tactics that are already practiced by insiders you can also enjoy success, saving big money and standing up for what's right.

2

Never Pay the First Bill

THE BILL FOR MY SEVENTEEN-YEAR-OLD son's treatment showed up a few weeks after his appointment. I had taken him to an urgent care in Little Rock, Arkansas, during a road trip. We had been swimming in a lake and he later had a bad earache. I knew it was probably just swimmer's ear, but after hearing some horror stories about flesh-eating bacteria that dwell in lakes, I wanted to be sure. The doctor cleaned out the ear and prescribed an antibiotic, and my son quickly recovered.

I paid my $40 insurance copayment—the out-of-pocket fee my plan made me pay up front—at the time of the visit. Now the urgent care's "request for payment" arrived in my mailbox, saying I owed $250. Under a heading that said IMPORTANT MESSAGE, the bill said, "The balance provided is your responsibility." It told me to pay promptly. Under "responsible party" it listed my name in all caps: MARSHALL ALLEN. The amount was due, and the deadline was looming. If I took this thing at face value I would be reaching for my checkbook or calling them to provide my credit card number.

When I scrutinized my $250 bill, I discovered it was flawed at its core. It was a bogus bill. The bill correctly named United-Healthcare as my insurance provider. But it said the portion paid by my insurance plan had been $0.00. That couldn't be right, I thought. I have an extremely expensive insurance plan that provides good benefits.

I called United. Nope, the insurance rep told me, the urgent care had not even submitted the claim. They needed to be billing my insurance company, not me. The bill listed a customer service number for the urgent care company, so I called, and a woman named Sandy told me they had submitted it, "but it doesn't look like it got processed correctly."

Sandy agreed to resubmit the bill. She told me to ignore the $250 bill her company had sent me. Problem solved. It took about ten minutes.

I felt relieved to discover the issue, but the error bugged me. What if I had trusted the bill and paid it? I'd be out $250! Sandy had not been concerned that her company sent me a bill for something I didn't owe. I asked her where their quality control broke down in their billing system. She wouldn't even agree that something *had* gone wrong: "I'm not going to say it's anybody's mistake," she told me.

Sandy didn't care how the mistake had happened. She certainly didn't take responsibility for it or pledge to correct it so it didn't happen again. Her blasé attitude about my bogus medical bill underscores why patients need to be on guard. Mistakes can get made every step of the way when it comes to billing patients. But they still hold us responsible for paying whatever amount they say we owe them, even if the bill is wrong. I could get sent to collections for failing to pay $250. Some clinics and hospitals will even sue patients for that amount.

The United States is suffering from an epidemic of bogus medical bills. Perhaps you are among the afflicted. Whether it's sloppiness, or haste or fraud or greed—or some combination—experts who review medical bills for a living say *most* of them contain some type of mistake. Somehow, the errors don't seem to work in the patient's favor. They always seem to require you to pay much more than you should. The inaccuracies aren't a new problem, though they have probably increased because electronic medical records have added so much cutting and pasting and clicking. I recently reviewed a record for an eight-year-old boy that said the patient did not know if "she" was pregnant. Um, I think we know the young boy was not pregnant.

If you've gotten a medical bill—whether large or small—don't panic. Take a deep breath. Do not pay it right away. You need to make sure it's not a bogus bill. Many are inaccurate. Many have unfair prices. Many have not been properly processed by your insurance plan. You need to be sure you're not getting ripped off. I'm going to walk you through the process in this chapter. The steps include obtaining an itemized medical bill, checking your insurance company's explanation of benefits (EOB), doing a price check, and asking for a discount.

The point is: You can't ignore these bills. You must check them for errors and get them corrected and reduced before they put you in debt, get sent to collections, and possibly harm your credit. The idea of inspecting medical bills probably sounds so boring and frustrating, or scary, that you want to throw this book under your bed. It may take you mere minutes to get a bogus bill resolved. It may take a few phone calls and follow-ups, or maybe an email or two. Or it could consume hours of your time and attention. You will need to muddle through some hassle and complexity. But fighting each bill could save you and your family a lot of money. So how much is your time worth? Reducing a bogus bill may be like paying yourself hundreds of dollars an hour—by protecting your own money. Also, there are other benefits to defending yourself. You could be spared from the downward spiral caused by debt and financial loss—and that may be even more valuable in the long run. And finally, identifying billing errors and refusing to pay for them provides accountability for the health care system. We've been paying for their sloppiness for decades. That changes now.

Bogus Bills Are Extremely Common

The mistakes and manipulations of medical records and bills come from a lot of sources. One source is out-of-network doctors and other medical providers who do not have agreed-upon rates with insurance companies. They charge outrageous fees and the insurer covers only a portion, leaving the balance of the bill for the patient. Your bills may include charges for services you didn't receive. They may overcharge for the care you did receive. You may get double billed for the same services. Your insurance company may not properly enter your information or apply your benefits. Or perhaps someone added the wrong diagnosis and procedure codes or patient information into your record.

Journalists routinely document the most outrageous and absurd medical bills. The headlines from the "Bill of the Month" project by the excellent reporters at Kaiser Health News capture the situation:[1] APPENDICITIS IS PAINFUL: ADD A $41,212 SURGERY BILL TO THE MISERY; FOR HER HEAD COLD, INSURER COUGHED UP $25,865; FIRST KIDNEY FAILURE: THEN A $540,842 BILL FOR DIALYSIS; and A YEAR AFTER SPINAL SURGERY A $94,031 BILL FEELS LIKE A BACK-BREAKER.

I've talked to medical bill reviewers who caught bogus bills for multiple thyroid or gallbladder removals or even more than one circumcision on the same patient on the same day. I remember a lively conversation I had with Missy Conley and Jeanne Woodward, who have battled on behalf of hundreds of patients who have been bogus billed. The two worked for Medliminal, a Virginia company that challenges erroneous and inflated medical bills on behalf of consumers in exchange for a share of the savings.

The two women excitedly one-upped each other with their favorite outrages. How about the two cases involving unnecessary pregnancy tests? One of the patients was eighty-two—decades past her childbearing years. The other involved a younger woman who no longer had a uterus. Another case involved an uninsured man who fell off his mountain bike and hurt his shoulder. The first responders pressured him to take an air ambulance to a hospital when it would have been faster for his friends to drive him. He got charged $44,000 for the whirlybird.

If there's a billing dispute it can take mere minutes or, in the extreme, months of phone calls and emails to get a case resolved, said Conley, who gained an insider's knowledge during years working for insurance companies.

The media and professional medical bill combatants highlight the most sensational examples. But most of the bogus medical bills won't make headlines. And the truth is, most of us have not been challenging them. The paperwork pours in and we get confused by the disjointed mess of bills, insurance documents, and random statements that are not considered bills, and we shove the stuff into a drawer or leave it in a pile on a countertop. This is the biggest mistake we can make.

So let's dig in. The methods described in this chapter can be applied to fight a bogus medical bill whether you've just received the initial bill, or have debt collectors calling, or have been sued. Similar principles apply to each situation.

The key is to start fighting right away.

Following Polson's Lead

We can take up this challenge by following our field generals, people like Crystal Polson, who have fought the system and won. With the right tactical moves and a lot of tenacity, we can beat back bogus bills.

When Crystal's five-year-old son Jack steered his Power Wheels rideable Jeep under a hammock it caught him in the face, crashing him to the ground and breaking his jaw.

Everything went well during the child's first visit to the emergency room, in September 2017 at St. Joseph's University Medical Center in Paterson, New Jersey. The oral surgeon saved some of Jack's teeth and stabilized his jaw with a wire, according to Crystal. The bills were accurate and paid by her insurance company with no hassle.

But a few weeks later, the wire became dislodged and Crystal had to take Jack to the same emergency room to have it repaired. She and Jack waited more than seven hours for the surgeon, who took one look at his mouth and announced that the work would have to be done the next day at a dental clinic. No one did any actual medical examination of the child. No medical services were provided. In fact, she said Jack spent most of the time snoozing.

This time when the bills arrived Polson could see an obvious problem. The bill included charges for a moderately complex medical examination that had supposedly been performed by a doctor and a nurse practitioner. The problem is: Those clinicians hadn't even seen Jack, she said. Crystal's insurance had already paid its portion, sticking her with about $323—for an examination that had never occurred. The hospital was about to learn that it was messing with the wrong parent.

Polson is a registered nurse and licensed nurse practitioner who works as a patient advocate to help others with similar cases. I find it darkly encouraging that the experts who work inside the medical industry are also getting burned by it. It shows there's not something wrong with the rest of us. Sometimes when things go wrong people blame us, or we blame ourselves, as if we were somehow at fault. That's not the case. The medical machine has just as much disregard for insiders like Polson as it does for the laypeople who don't know the system. The difference is that an insider like Polson is more likely to know how to fight the system. That's why it's important to take her lead when it comes to learning how to win these battles.

Polson said she probably catches errors in about 80 percent of the medical bills she reviews for her clients. So that's the first thing she does before paying her own medical bills. Her battle against the inaccurate bill for Jack's phantom examination is a guide for the rest of us. When you get your first bill, realize that it may be wrong or you may be able to negotiate for a lower price.

STEP 1: Obtain an itemized bill.

Most medical bills merely sum up how much the patient is expected to pay, without laying out the individual charges that make up the total. That would be like your grocery store telling you to pay a lump sum for all your groceries instead of telling you how much you paid for bread, milk, eggs, and other individual items. Patients have a right to a detailed breakdown that includes an explanation of each service provided and the proper billing code used for each charge. And we need this to make sure that each charge accurately reflects what happened.

You're looking for specific codes that lay out the charges for physician services. Doctors and other types of medical providers bill with current procedural terminology, or CPT, codes. Hospitals use international classification of diseases, or ICD-10-PCS, codes for the procedures they bill. The definition and description for each code is available online.

Shelley Safian is one of my favorite people to learn from when it comes to the intricacies of medical billing. She's written multiple medical billing textbooks and teaches courses on the subject. She said CPT codes will be five numbers all in a row, like 12345. Sometimes the five-digit number might be followed by a hyphen and two more numbers or letters. For example, 99213-95. The 95 modifier means the office visit was conducted via telemedicine.

The itemized invoice you receive will show charges for each billing code that are like a manufacturer's suggested retail price, the MSRP. The main thing to keep in mind is that nobody is expected to pay these sticker prices. Insurance companies are supposed to negotiate discounts off the list prices. Uninsured patients might be told to pay them, but they should negotiate for a better deal.

To understand the codes, just Google the code number with the term "medical billing code" and read the descriptions. It takes a minute to understand them, but it's not rocket science. You can do it! Or perhaps a friend or family member can help you. To understand terminology, you may also want to buy a copy of *Merriam Webster's Medical Dictionary* and consult the website medlineplus.gov, which is written in layman's terms and published by the U.S. National Library of Medicine. Looking up terms online will also help you learn.

STEP 2: If you are insured, examine your insurance company's explanation of benefits.

Your insurance company should send you an explanation of benefits, or EOB, that breaks down the charges, how the plan paid for the care you received, and how much of the charge is being passed on to the patient.

Safian provided the following example of an insurance company's explanation of benefits:

Provided Service	Provider Billed Plan	Total Cost (Allowed Amount)	Plan Paid	Coinsurance/ Copay	Deductible	Your Share
06/30/2020 Billing Code: 99214	$324.00	109.18	$109.18	$0.00	$0.00	$0.00
06/30/2020 Billing Code: 99080	$0.01	$0.00	$0.00	$0.00	$0.00	$0.00

Here's what the columns mean, starting from the left side:

Column 1—DATE. The date is the date the service occurred. The billing code is the code that describes the service the medical provider says the patient received. In this case, the CPT code 99214 shows the charge is for an office visit for an established patient.

Column 2—PROVIDER CHARGE AMOUNT. This is like the manufacturer's suggested retail price on a car. No one is expected to pay the amount, and it can be whatever charge they want. Often it's many times more than what they would accept for the service, because the insurance company wants to be able to say it got the patient a discount.

Column 3—ALLOWED AMOUNT. This is the maximum that the insurance plan has said it will pay for this particular CPT code.

Column 4—PLAN PAID. This is what the insurance plan paid

to the provider. So the plan paid $109.18 even though the doctor billed $324.00.

Column 5—COINSURANCE. The coinsurance is based on a percentage of the allowed amount that the patient must pay. This is explained in your insurance plan documents. You often will see this as 80/20 or something similar. That means the insurance plan will pay 80 percent of the allowed amount and the patient must pay 20 percent. On this EOB, the coinsurance is $0.00, but if it was 20 percent, then it would read $21.84, and in that case the "plan paid" would be $87.34.

The copay is a fixed number that the patient must always pay for that encounter. It may change determined by the location. For example, the patient may need to pay $20 at the physician's office, but $50 at an urgent care clinic and $250 at a hospital emergency room.

Column 6—DEDUCTIBLE. This is an amount that must be paid, out of the patient's pocket, before insurance policy benefits will be applied. In this instance, the deductible amount says $0.00, because the patient had no deductible. It might also be $0.00 if you already met your deductible. But if the deductible was $100, for example, then the patient would pay the $100 and the plan would pay $9.18.

Column 7—YOUR SHARE. This is what the patient should actually pay.

Yes, EOBs can be confusing! But Safian insists that patients need to understand EOBs, and they should only pay their medical bills based on the EOB. Check the EOB to make sure the charges are accurate and that they were accurately run through your plan. Then pay based on the "Your Share" amount. The EOBs may vary in layout from one company to another, but the terms are standard. Safian said it's also important for patients to read any notations that explain things like why an insurer might have denied payment for a particular service.

If you have questions about a charge or denial, Safian said you should pick up the phone and call your insurance company. The customer service number should be on your insurance card. The insurance representatives are incredibly helpful, she said, and will help you root out any inappropriate charges submitted by a doctor or hospital. They may also help you identify whether the charges were even submitted to your health plan, as I found out with my bogus bill for $250.

STEP 3: If necessary, obtain the relevant medical records.

It's your legal right to obtain your medical records, which are required to document every test or treatment the patient received. They can be obtained by calling your hospital or doctor and asking for whoever handles medical records. They should be able to send them to you electronically, and while some states may allow them to charge you, you should ask them to waive any charges. You don't have to tell them that you want the records to challenge the bill. It's a good idea for you to have the records regardless, in case you ever need to show a future doctor the type of care that was provided.

There's a saying about medical records: "If it's not documented, it didn't happen." The billing codes are supposed to come straight from the interpretation of the medical records, so examine the records to see if they document every charge that's on your itemized bill. If the charge isn't documented in your medical record, you should contest it. Refuse to pay anything that's not documented in the records—because if it's not documented they should not be billing for it in the first place. Be especially on the lookout for upcoding, which I'll discuss next.

STEP 4: Examine the itemized bills and the medical records to see if both reflect the care the patient *actually* received.

Crystal Polson immediately saw problems. One doctor bill for the visit had the CPT code 99283, which is used to bill a level 3 emergency services examination. But Jack hadn't been examined by anyone. Plus, the levels range from 1, for the quickest exam, to 5, for the most complex. It's easy to look up a description of these codes online. A 99283 billing code requires an expanded, problem-focused history to be taken of the patient, an expanded examination and medical decision making of moderate complexity. It results in a higher payment because it's for a patient with a complex problem.

Polson said the code didn't come close to accurately describing the reality of her emergency room visit with Jack. The medical records said the physician performed a head-to-toe, comprehensive physical. "That certainly did not happen," Polson wrote to the hospital in an email. Improper documentation drives up health care costs and raises questions about professionalism and ethics, she said in the email. This type of upcoding, using a code that exaggerates the complexity of a case, is one of the most common ways patients get ripped off. Medical providers get paid much more for each level of care they provide. It's also a major source of fraud. If a doctor or hospital claims the care they provided was more complicated than it was, we end up paying more.

Polson contested the bill to the hospital, but patients can also reach out to the clinician involved and ask them to adjust the medical code so that it's accurate. Then the bill can be resubmitted to the insurance carrier for proper payment.

STEP 5: Make sure your insurance plan properly paid the bill.

Insurance companies autopay almost all of the bills that come in from doctors and hospitals. They do not typically examine whether the care was appropriate. They merely check to see if the medical biller accurately completed the claim form, by including the right patient information and diagnosis and procedure codes and other details to explain what happened. This lack of scrutiny allows billing errors and fraud to run rampant.

The lax claims processing by carriers can lead to other costly mistakes. For example, under the Affordable Care Act all insurance plans are required to cover, at no cost to the patient, certain preventive services for adults—like vaccines, breast cancer screening every year or two for women over forty, and colorectal cancer screening for patients ages fifty to seventy-five. The services should be coded as preventive and the insured patient should pay nothing—even if they haven't met their annual deductible.[2] But these services often don't get coded as preventive, which means the cost gets passed on to the patient. It happens too frequently and it's an easy one for us to catch as patients. But we must be vigilant to see how things got coded and paid, or not paid, by our insurance carrier.

Polson appealed her inaccurate and potentially fraudulent bill twice to her insurer. The carrier rejected both her appeals. It didn't surprise her that the insurer would side with the medical provider rather than the patient. That's common. As I have said, the insurance companies often treat the doctors and hospitals like their customers, not the patients. The insurance companies need to keep the clinicians happy so they will stay in their networks. And if medical facilities and providers overcharge the insurers, so be it. The carriers can just raise premiums the next year to make patients fund whatever money they need. "A couple thousand dollars off their back is no sweat," Polson said of the insurers. "It's not their money. It's our money."

Thus, the insurer blindly paid its portion and passed the rest, $323.01, on to Polson.

STEP 6: Make sure the bill is priced fairly.

Patients—or their loved ones, like in Polson's case—agree to pay for the care that's provided. But that does not mean the medical provider can charge them exorbitant rates. She said she likes to use HealthcareBluebook.com or FairHealthConsumer.org to see if the prices are fair. The Bluebook site gathers payment information from employers who fund their own health plans and publishes what it calls its fair price for a service or procedure. The Fair Health site does something similar, but its data comes from what insurers pay. If you have the itemized statement with the billing codes you can easily plug the codes into each website to get a price comparison. It also may be possible to get the Medicare rates, although non-Medicare patients should expect to pay more than the Medicare prices.[3] I also recommend calling other nearby health care providers and use the billing codes to ask for the cash price for that service, where you can.

If you're dealing with a hospital, you may also be able to check its website and the sites for other nearby hospitals for their prices. The federal government now requires hospitals to post many prices, though their compliance has been hit or miss. But make sure you check.

One comparison you could look for is what the industry calls its usual, customary, and reasonable price—the amount someone would reasonably be expected to pay in your area. It's called the UCR for short, and it's a formal term.[4] There's a good chance the UCR is still higher than what you should be paying, but at least it's another benchmark for you to make a comparison with what you are being asked to pay.

In Polson's case there should have been no price because the exam hadn't happened at all.

STEP 7: Negotiate. See if there's a financial assistance policy.

Polson said patients should try to reach the supervisor of the billing department and should not hesitate to go all the way up the chain of command to the CEO.

Safian said you can write a letter to the doctor or hospital and include the research you've done as attachments. That takes some of the emotion out of the problem and can allow time for the medical provider to make the adjustment. Send the letter to the president or CEO of the hospital or physician group. The top executive can always hand it off to someone in the billing department.

Polson said she is almost always able to get the bill reduced, and sometimes by huge amounts. Other experts have told me the same. One time Polson said she got a pregnancy test that had been billed at $1,200 reduced to $90, just by asking.

You can also ask whether the provider has a financial assistance policy, which could result in a sliding scale discount, based on your income. Many people qualify, and discounts can range from 20 percent to 90 percent. You can look up hospital financial assistance policies on the website ClinicPriceCheck.com, where data scientist Joanne Rodrigues has compiled them for most of the hospitals in the country. The policies are more generous than people think, Rodrigues said. For example, a family of five making $100,000 could qualify for up to a 90 percent discount at some hospitals, depending on the size of their bills compared with their income. Other discounts are less generous, and they will depend on a variety of circumstances. But the point is: Check out these policies. If you're low income you likely qualify for a discount, and even if you make good money you may still be eligible.

A prompt payment discount could also be available if you're able to pay off your bill as a lump sum. If you're covered by a self-funded plan—which means your employer pays the medical costs for your health plan, not an insurance company—your employer's human resources department may also be able to help. But unfortunately, Polson said, the HR employees often don't know any more than the employees.

If the charge is for something that clearly never happened, and no one will correct it, or you've been overcharged and they won't budge, you can play hardball. Depending on how egregious the problem is, you could tell the doctor that you will be filing a complaint for fraud against his or her medical license if the charge is not corrected. Providing this level of individual accountability may be even more effective than going after the institution.

Polson filed complaints with the New Jersey medical examiner's office, her insurance company's fraud department, the New Jersey Department of Insurance, and the state Department of Health and Human Services. They said they don't deal with medical bills, but she convinced them it was a case of possible fraud and filing a false report. Each of them responded by saying what's written in the chart must be taken at face value. But bringing in the external accountability could create more incentive for the hospital or medical provider to deal with you fairly.

The point is, the prices on your bill are not as hard and fast as you might expect. There may be various ways they can be reduced, so you should explore getting a better deal if you're getting overcharged or are unable to afford them.

STEP 8: Go public.

Tagging the medical provider on Twitter or Facebook and calling out their unfair billing practices can be effective. You could also find a journalist like me who is interested in these types of stories. But be forewarned, we get buried in so many calls and emails from patients who need to get their story told that we can't always return them. We also must be selective about which stories we pursue. We look for cases that are extremes, or that expose patterns of misconduct, or that have broad potential for reform. Things need to be on the record and documented. Also, we need to independently verify the story, so we need to see medical and billing records and get the patient's permission to contact the medical providers. We can report on only a fraction of the legitimate stories that need to be covered. But then again, we are always on the hunt for these cases of wrongdoing. We want to expose them, so reach out to us. If you'd like to share your story with me, fill out the form on my website, marshallallen.com. I'm especially interested in hearing your story if you've been victorious so that we can share your winning tactics with others. But also let me know if you need help and I will see what I can do.

STEP 9: Seek advice from other patients who have fought their bills.

The hive mind of the internet is a tremendous resource for patients who are up against the medical industry. Do a search on Facebook for groups dedicated to fighting back against the high cost of health care. Often anyone can join and post a question about how to handle a bogus bill. The communities can also be places for encouragement and support. People who have suffered from harm related to medical care can find encouragement and resources in the Patient Safety Action Network Community on Facebook.[5] I started this patient safety group with my *ProPublica* colleagues in 2012 and moderated for six years before turning it over to the Patient Safety Action Network advocate group.

STEP 10: Consider hiring a patient advocate.

Professional patient advocates charge a fee, so you may not be able to afford one, or the case might not be worth paying to resolve. But depending on the case, you might need the experience and tenacity they bring. You could check out the National Association of Health-care Advocacy consultants, at www.nahac.com, or go to the Advo Connection Directory, which is online at advoconnection.com. Advo Connection has a helpful guide for interviewing and hiring a patient advocate.[6] It's important to interview the advocate to understand the person's credentials, the charges and references. A professional advocate is probably worth considering only if you're fighting bills that are thousands of dollars or extremely complicated because of a lengthy hospital stay.

STEP 11: Sue them in small claims court.

I will go into detail about how to do this in chapter five. Small claims courts have limits depending on where you live. But they offer a big advantage to patients because they don't require an attorney. Once you've done your homework and understand the bogus nature of your medical bills, you can provide that documentation when you file your legal complaint against whoever is billing you. Remember, you can sue only for the amount that you determine you are being overcharged plus court costs.

After months of phone calls and emails, Polson won what she calls a partial victory. She lost her fight to get her insurance company to reject the bill, but she did get the hospital to waive the $323 it had been demanding from her. She felt relieved, but ultimately her fight wasn't about the money. "I hope by now you know this is not about how much money you are claiming I owe," she wrote in one email to hospital officials. "I can afford to pay my bills. Unfortunately, many folks can't, and this is why I will continue to persist."

I contacted the hospital to get their side of the story. They wouldn't talk to me about it and would say only that the situation with Polson got resolved.

Polson said that each step of the process may feel like a wrestling match. "It takes determination and tenacity—not giving up," she told me.

But that's how it is with a fight. We can't roll over. The medical industry has behaved as if it's entitled to our money and can take it even if they are wrong. Patients are just starting to stand up for themselves, so we should expect the industry to resist. But we have the numbers on our side. If more of us demand fair and accurate billing it may press them to stop the predatory practices. It won't be worth their while to battle all of us. We need to create enough pain for them that we make it in their best interest to stop the abuse.

If you have the resources—as many individuals and employers do—you can get more aggressive. You may be able to hire an attorney to defend yourself, like Jim Farley did.

Farley is the ultimate medical industry insider. He owns a third-party administrator in Cleveland, Ohio. That's a company that processes claims and administers health plans for self-funded employers—those employers who fund their own health benefits, as opposed to paying a premium to a traditional insurance company to cover the costs. He fights bogus bills on behalf of the employers who are his clients, so naturally he knew what to do when he faced one himself. He's the type of battle-worn guide who's blazing a trail for the rest of us.

Farley broke his shoulder skiing on the last day of 2013 at Holiday Valley Resort in Ellicottville, New York. He went to an orthopedic specialist when he came off the hill, who X-rayed and reset the shoulder. The bill came to $700 and he paid it. The specialist told him to keep the shoulder stabilized for about six weeks and then go to a doctor to get orders for physical therapy.

He went for follow-up to an orthopedic practice near his home in Lakewood, which is part of the Cleveland metro area. He received an X-ray and referral for physical therapy. But when he got the bill, he saw they had added a code and a charge for resetting the shoulder. But that didn't make sense. The doctor in New York had already reset his shoulder when he came off the ski slope. Farley disputed the bill with the hometown orthopedic group. He urged them to remove the charge, but they wouldn't back off.

The dispute went on for months and culminated with the orthopedic group suing Farley for $2,102 on December 17, 2014, in Lakewood Municipal Court. The physician group attached a copy of the medical bills as an exhibit and claimed Farley had failed to pay the balance.

Farley wouldn't have it. He hired an attorney and countersued the orthopedic group for fraud—billing him for services they never provided.

Farley's countersuit forced the orthopedic group to give in. They both agreed to drop the case, with Farley owing nothing for the trumped-up medical bills. In addition, Farley required the orthopedic group to make a $100 donation to a local community center that provides mental health services.

Farley urges other patients to fight their bogus bills. "If you know how to work the system you can overcome these things."

He's right—and that's the purpose of this book, to equip you and inspire you to fight back, so you can stand up for yourself and save money. Let's start a wave of patients who refuse to back down from bogus medical bills.

Now that you understand the basics of fighting a bill, let's turn to a specific issue in medical billing: insurance denials. Your insurance company may flat-out refuse to pay for the care that you or a family member needs. If that's the case, you're facing an urgent battle. But fear not, in the next chapter I'll introduce you to a guide who can show you the path forward.

3

The Insurance Warrior's Guide to Winning Your Appeal

HOLLY FREULER'S ABDOMEN WAS OVERRUN with a rare form of cancer, and she needed the doctor who had the expertise to save her life.

Freuler lives near Orlando, Florida, and at the time worked as a clinical analyst for the Florida Hospital chain, which is now part of a large health system called AdventHealth. The doctor everyone pointed to as the expert in her disease operated out of Washington, D.C. That's where she ran into a problem. Her employer's health plan said it wouldn't cover the surgery because the specialist wasn't in its network, meaning he didn't have agreed-upon rates with the plan.

Freuler's insurance company, which processed the bills and administered the health plan, told her it would cover the care she needed only if she stayed with the in-network doctors and hospitals that already had agreed-upon rates. The problem is, those doctors didn't have the expertise to save her life. She needed to go out of network but was told it would cost her more than $100,000. She had to persuade her health plan to enter a single-case contract with the specialist so she wouldn't get stuck with the bill.

You might have encountered a similar situation. Your health plan may be blocking you from getting the care you need, claiming it's experimental or not available in its network of medical providers, even though that network may be extremely narrow, meaning not many medical providers are in it. Insurers control costs by steering you to the doctors they have under contract, whether or not that's the best medical provider for you. Insurers may reject coverage for medications or treatments before you receive them. And if you have already undergone care or received a medication or treatment, insurers may refuse to pay for it.

Your health plans give you the right to appeal any denial of care. But you need to bring your A game. You may not get a fair hearing. It's too easy for the health plan to take your appeal and swat it back in your face. Fortunately, we can turn to Laurie Todd, aka the Insurance Warrior, to coach us through the process, so we have the best shot at success.

Let's look at how the Insurance Warrior guided Freuler through her appeal. Her story has numerous insights that you could apply to an appeal of your own. Freuler works in the health care industry, so she was more equipped than many patients to take on the appeal. But she felt overwhelmed. She was a young woman, just thirty-three years old. But she suffered from a rare cancer called cystic mesothelioma that was filling her insides with thousands of tiny cancerous cysts. She scoured medical studies and spoke to doctors and knew not just anyone could save her life. Dr. Paul Sugarbaker in Washington, D.C., had treated thousands of cases similar to hers. But she had to get her health insurance plan on board.

People who live with ongoing health problems or who get hit

with something dire like cancer often turn to online communities for help. While participating in an online patient group Freuler came across Todd, who years before her had suffered from late-stage appendix cancer. Todd's health plan had also rejected her treatment, but she fought back and won an appeal with thorough research and a shrewd campaign to convince her health plan's decision makers. Word of Todd's success got out in the online patient groups and she started helping other patients work through insurance appeals. She found she was good at it. Soon she became known as the Insurance Warrior.

In the past fifteen years the Insurance Warrior has orchestrated appeals for 239 patients and counting. She calls herself a writer and insurance strategist and her approach combines legal reasoning, psychology, and storytelling—infused with an intense concentration of bravado. She writes the appeal in the voice of the patient—she calls them her helpees—and coordinates the campaign to get it approved. The patient sends out the appeal on a Sunday night so it's at the top of people's email inboxes when they start their week. The patient starts working the phones Monday morning, making personal calls to decision makers. Todd expects to have it approved by Tuesday afternoon, two days later. "The last three appeals we won in two hours," she told me.

Todd charges a fee, but it's a modest amount given what's at stake and her expertise. By her count, she has lost fewer than ten appeals. This chapter will highlight her methods, and you might think it sounds totally overwhelming. I get that. But your physical and financial health might depend on getting your insurance plan to cover something you need. To give yourself the best shot you need to understand how insurance companies or employer-sponsored health plans operate, and how they are trying to steer you so things work out to their advantage. It will be a struggle, but you may not have any other option.

Plus, in fighting the insurance companies, Todd has gleaned so many insights to show how the system works against us. And her radical approach to taking on the system reframes the traditional way of looking at this problem.

This chapter is a high-level overview of Todd's approach to appeals. She details her method in her book *Approved: Win Your Insurance Appeal in 5 Days*.[1] I spoke to patients whom Todd guided through the process and also those who won their appeal by using the book as a guide. If you're facing a high-stakes appeal, you must read her book.

Insurance companies and employers don't operate in good faith when they consider appeals, Todd said, so patients should not let them control how they make their appeal. Patients need to be renegades. "In a bad faith process, you should do the opposite of what they suggest," she told me.

Know your opponent: Are you in a self-funded or fully insured plan?

Freuler didn't realize it until she had to make her appeal, but her employer had a self-funded health benefit plan. That means her employer, Florida Hospital, funded the plan, instead of having an insurance company take responsibility for the costs. Most of the working Americans who get their benefits through their employer are in self-funded plans. Organizations with more than two hundred or so employees are most likely to self-fund, but it's sometimes done with companies as small as fifty or one hundred people. Self-funding makes sense because it gives employers more control over how the money is spent. And if they're smart about it they can provide better coverage for a lot less money. Self-funded employers typically hire an insurance company to administer the plan, but the carrier is acting as a third-party administrator. The plan utilizes the insurer's network of doctors and hospitals and uses the carrier to process its claims and run the health plan. The insurer also rejects requests from patients and might be involved in appeals. But the insurer does not set the policies. Those are established by the employer's benefits department.

In other cases, employers purchase a plan from a health insurer. That's called a fully insured plan and this is more typically what people think of when they hear the term "health insurance." The insurance company takes in premiums to cover medical costs, but ultimately bears the risk if those costs run higher than what it obtained in premiums. If someone buys an individual plan, that's also going to be fully insured.

Patients need to know whether they are in a self-funded or fully insured plan because they are regulated in different ways. The federal government's Department of Labor oversees self-funded plans. State regulators, like insurance commissioners or departments, oversee fully insured plans. That means appeals take a different route, depending on the type of plan. If you're in a fully insured plan you will go through your insurer, and perhaps through an external review process provided by your state insurance department. If you're in a self-funded plan, your employer needs to be involved in your appeal. You might have a better chance because the employer has greater flexibility and you have an established relationship. The employee might have some leverage. On the other hand, it puts patients in an uncomfortable position when their employment is tied to their health care, and the employer is denying them the care they need.

Patients in fully insured plans should check their state laws and regulations for anything that could help them with their case. Health insurers are careful to comply with any state laws and regulations.[2] So you want to quote your state's laws to your fully insured plan when making your appeal, Todd said. Every state law is different, so check your location, but Todd points out in her book the four types of state regulations that could apply to your case:

- State regulators often require insurers to use qualified doctors to do any reviews of a patient's appeal. Find out who the doctor is who reviewed your case for the insurance company and question whether he or she has the expertise to rule on your unique and complex case. Chances are that the doctor is not specially qualified. Insurance companies are also not known for hiring the best of the best when it comes to physicians.
- Some states say the doctor providing the treatment rules, which means your personal physician can overrule the insurance company. That's good, because if the insurer says your treatment should not be covered, but your personal physician says it should be, then you can win your appeal.
- States may require insurers to provide an adequate network of doctors. In Todd's home state, Washington, insurers are required to cover an out-of-network service as if it was in network if the service is not available in its network.[3] Those are called network adequacy laws. Check if your state has one.
- Many states also require insurers to make exceptions for certain qualified out-of-network medical providers. If your medical condition requires special expertise, then you can argue that you must go to a specific doctor and state law says it must be covered. Cite that law.

If you're feeling intimidated about finding the right state law or regulation, Todd says you should call your insurance commissioner or insurance department. These state regulators are supposed to be serving the needs of the public, and if you call them to ask for help in a friendly way they are likely to assist you. When you call, try using Todd's favorite line to ensure you find the right person to help you: "I need to ask a question about a specific health insurance regulation." She said that statement will get you transferred to someone who has the specialized knowledge you need. I think that's great advice. I've had a lot of conversations with people who work in the bowels of health care regulator offices and other medical institutions. They often enjoy having a conversation with mere mortals like us because they get to help and share their expertise.

So remember, if you're in a fully insured plan, use the state regulations to your advantage.

Most of Todd's appeals involve self-funded plans. She loves to take them on because she believes the employers are hiding behind the insurance carriers they hire as administrators. Employers don't want their employees to know that they are the ones doing the medical decision making, she said to me. They are trying to hand off their financial responsibility and liability. That means the employers can be skittish, so she said they need to be intimidated with a light hand. Come on too strong and they will resist. Apply subtle leverage and they will comply. "Appeals are not about information, they're about intimidation," Todd told me, sounding like the ancient Chinese military strategist Sun Tzu in *The Art of War*. "But it has to be subtle or they're going to push back."

Health plans will often guarantee a patient the right to appeal a rejection to an independent medical reviewer. With fully insured plans this process often takes place through the office of the state insurance regulator. It's possible to win this way at least some of the time. I downloaded the outcomes for patients who appealed their insurance company denials and found the decision of the insurer gets overturned during the independent medical review process about half the time.[4] So a patient can go this route if it's relevant, but Todd doesn't recommend it. She doesn't believe the independent reviews are truly independent. Things are always stacked in favor of the insurer, so she said patients should just skip any peer review or independent reviews and proceed with their own appeal.

What if you're reading this chapter and you've already lost your appeal? Insurance plans generally limit the number of times a patient can make an appeal. But remember the Insurance Warrior's rule—do the opposite. You get as many appeals as you say you do. Just make sure you "don't step in the same cow pie twice" by filing the same crappy appeal you filed the first time, Todd writes in her book.[5]

Are you covered by a self-funded plan? Stand up to your employer.

If you're in a self-funded health plan, the idea of challenging your employer puts almost any worker in a difficult position. But it needs to happen if an employee or their family member is going to appeal to get the care they need. These appeals could mean life or death. And remember: Your employer is not necessarily your friend. Lauren Bard found this out the hard way. Bard is a nurse for a Southern California hospital run by Dignity Health—a massive health care chain with the tagline "Hello Humankindness." Dignity refused to pay the cost of the care needed by Sadie, Bard's premature baby, because of a technicality. Bard had called the insurance carrier that administered the self-funded plan right after the baby was born to sign the child up on the plan. But Dignity said she was supposed to have signed the baby up for coverage through its website within thirty-one days of the birth. She didn't follow this particular protocol in time and they claimed she was too late. Her employer, via the insurer administering the plan, stuck her with the bill for a three-month stay in the neonatal intensive care unit. About a week before I spoke to Bard, in the fall of 2019, she got hit with a medical bill so big it made her body go numb. In bold block letters it said "AMOUNT DUE: $898,984.57."

Dignity is one of the largest health systems in the country, with services in twenty-two states. The massive nonprofit self-funds its benefits, meaning it bears the cost of bills like Sadie's. And it doesn't appear to be short on cash. In 2018 the organization reported $6.6 billion in net assets and paid its CEO $11.9 million in reportable compensation, according to tax filings. That same year more than two dozen Dignity executives earned more than $1 million in compensation, records show.

Dignity is also a religious organization that says its mission is to further "the healing ministry of Jesus." Surely, Bard remembered thinking, they would show her compassion.

With the specter of the bills hanging over her, Bard literally begged Dignity to change its mind in multiple phone calls, working her way up to supervisors. She thought she'd enrolled Sadie by calling the insurer, she told them. It was an innocent mistake. She had also been in the hospital for days due to complications from the birth. Dignity didn't care.

Dignity rejected both of Bard's appeals, saying the government didn't allow it to make any exceptions to its rules. But when I heard about Bard's case I knew that wasn't true. Self-funded plans can always make exceptions. The law just requires them to make exceptions in a way that's equal to all participants in the plan. The law also allows them to give greater exceptions to people with adverse health factors—like the medical complications Bard had to deal with.

Sadie's total hospital tab was nearing $1 million and climbing when I talked to her. "I'll either work the rest of my life or file for bankruptcy," she told me.

I contacted someone from Dignity to write a story for Pro-Publica about the case.[6] I knew the employer could make an exception for her.

Sure enough, the next day, Bard got a call from the senior vice president of operations for Dignity Southern California, who apologized and said she'd heard about the situation from the organization's media team and would help. Two days later, Dignity added Sadie to the plan, retroactive to her birth date. It covered the bills.

"We based this new decision on certain extenuating and compelling circumstances, which, in all likelihood prohibited you from enrolling your newborn daughter within the Plan's required 31-day enrollment period," the letter said.

Right—she had been telling Dignity about her extenuating circumstances for the entire year, through two appeals.

Bard's story has a happy ending. Her bills for Sadie—whom she calls her million-dollar baby—got wiped clean. But it happened only because I got involved and we put them on blast. The company realized it would be held accountable publicly for what had happened, so it reversed course.

Most of you don't have a journalist waiting in the wings. That means you should learn to write and win your own appeals, even if it means taking on your employer. It might be uncomfortable, but your life and financial security might depend on it. And the Insurance Warrior shows how it can be done.

Make your case with evidence and social pressure—not emotion.

One of the Insurance Warrior's savviest moves is to steer patients away from making appeals based on emotion. I've seen this many times myself when patients are being harmed by their health plan's denial. You can hardly blame them. Their lives are being ruined, so it's natural to feel upset. I would be crying, too! But you won't win your appeal by plaintive begging to show the suffering and death caused by denying care to you or your child or spouse or the grandparent whom everyone loves. This is a cold and heartless system that's dictated by compliance with laws and rules and guidelines and regulations and other contractual language. Thus, winning your appeal is done by boldly showing how your employer and insurer have violated the contract they had with the patient. It's about tearing them to shreds with evidence and hanging them with their own fine print.

Your health plan's documents say it will provide the medically necessary care you or your insured loved one needs. It's a contractual arrangement. Thus, the appeal needs to be a merciless and matter-of-fact thrashing of the breach of contract. The appeal needs to overpower the employer and insurer and not let up until they tap out by approving your demands.

Todd starts each case with a deep dive into the scientific literature and by identifying and getting contact information for the top executives for the employer and the insurer administering the plan. It's similar to the work I do as an investigative reporter—just digging and digging for nuggets of valuable information. She wants to know the names, phone numbers, and email addresses of the most influential people she can find and she will spend hours searching for them. Yes, this is hard work. It takes tenacity. But you've got to fight to win.

Once she's done her research, Todd weaves her findings into a detailed appeal document—Freuler's came to sixty-two pages[7]— laid out like a legal brief. She writes it in the patient's voice, as if you had hired an expert to write your résumé. Then she helps the patient wage an urgent campaign of social pressure at the highest levels of the employer and insurer to push them to approve the treatment. "I'm the puppet master," she told me, "the power behind the throne."

That sounds like grandiose exaggeration until you see how it works. Consider how she launched Freuler's appeal. First, she waited until the last minute. An insurer or employer might give thirty days for an appeal, but Todd says you should wait to send your appeal until the last minute—like within days of your scheduled medical procedure—so it lands with a sense of urgency.

The title of every Insurance Warrior appeal is the same: **URGENT EXPEDITED REQUEST FOR RECONSIDERATION.** Yes—it's in bold and ALL CAPS. Yes—it's underlined. The decision makers need to have it come to the top of their priority list, she says, not bury it down in the slush pile.

Todd finds the names of about twenty top executives for the employer and insurance carrier and copies all of them, as well as the names of some board members or other outside authorities— the "outside eyes"—that lend a sense of importance and accountability. Freuler addressed her appeal to the Florida Hospital appeals department and copied fourteen big shots, including the president and other executives from AdventHealth, which owns the hospital, and the chairman and CEO and other executives from Coventry Health Care, the insurance carrier that administered the plan. She even threw in an attorney from the Department of Justice.

Todd doesn't expect the heavy hitters to actually read through the appeal document. But she wants everyone who considers the appeal to at least think the higher-ups might be looking. The point is to raise the perceived importance of the appeal in the eyes of anyone handling it. That way it will not be ignored. Plus, all it takes is one of those decision makers to give the nod and the whole appeal gets approved. "Who you send an appeal to is more important than what you say," Todd explained to me. "If you write a crappy two-page snivelgram and send it to a carefully curated list of all these secret decision makers, to their personal emails, you might actually win. But if you write a brilliantly crafted, fact- and science-filled fifty-two-page research paper and send it to the P.O. box listed for the employee benefits department—you've lost."

Even on the phone, speaking from her home in Kirkland, Washington, Todd is a force. I kept taking notes: "Access is power," she said, continuing her lecture. "Everything I do is about leverage and strategy. I have to find every bit of tiny leverage I can find and fluff it up into a giant thing."

Build a meticulous case.

Freuler needed her employer to pay for her to see Sugarbaker, the Washington, D.C., specialist, for a radical form of treatment known as cytoreductive surgery and hyperthermic intraperitoneal chemotherapy—HIPEC for short. The surgery requires a massive abdominal incision and the careful removal of hundreds or thousands of cancerous cysts, followed by pouring liquid chemotherapy into the open cavity to treat the microscopic cancer cells that remain after the operation. It's extreme and not many doctors do it, but the evidence shows it works.

Freuler did her research before the appeal, using Todd's questions to interview the insurer's in-network doctors to show that they didn't have the expertise to provide her with the care she needed. She took notes during the conversations and Todd incorporated the interviews into the appeal to show that the treatment Freuler needed wasn't available in network. Freuler also called her own organization's benefits department and took notes, to show they didn't have any good options for her.

"What can I do about my cancer?" she asked her benefits representative.

"I've never heard of that," the rep said of her disease.

"Who can I go to for treatment?" she asked the benefits department.

"I have no idea," her rep told her.

Todd has used this tactic so many times she has a name for it: the Runaround Story. Freuler was showing that her own health plan was not providing her with the coverage she needed to save her life. It was giving her the Runaround. That's violating the heart of her health benefits contract, Todd said. It all goes in the appeal. Hang them with their own words.

Todd's appeal for Freuler cited studies that showed the rationale for the treatment she needed. She showed that Sugarbaker had performed more than 2,000 of the procedures and had kept careful statistics showing his success and published 475 peer-reviewed medical studies. She showed that in 159 cases insurance companies have covered the procedure. And in cases where the doctor was out of network, the carrier made an exception and fully funded the treatment by writing a single-case contract with the clinician. Each case showing precedent—all 159 of them—included the name of the patient, the surgery date, the diagnosis, and the insurance company that paid for the treatment. Todd said precedent is especially important because if the insurer or other insurers have paid for something multiple times, there is no excuse for them not paying for it again.

Todd wrapped up the written appeal by using the health plan's own definition of "medical necessity" to prove that Freuler's case was medically necessary. The case is appropriate and necessary—in other words, consistent with professionally recognized standards, not primarily for the convenience of the patient or physician—

providing the most appropriate level of service and enabling reasonable progress in treatment. She pointed out that it's also cost effective, because it's less expensive for everyone if Freuler heals and doesn't have a prolonged sickness. "Bad outcomes? Very costly. Good outcomes? Very cost effective."

Work the phones to pressure decision makers to take your side.

Todd and Freuler role-played the phone campaign in advance. Freuler took the day off the Monday morning after sending the appeal to the top decision makers so she could work the phones, under Todd's direction. Starting early in the morning, she called every executive copied on the appeal document to make sure they gave it a close look. She had three goals—as outlined in the Insurance Warrior's book: Make sure each of them got the appeal, make sure they look at it, and make sure they say when she will have the decision.

As a nurse, Freuler felt intimidated cold-calling her health system's top executives. But her life depended on this showdown. She was going to bring the fight to them.

"Who do you think you are calling this number," she recalls an assistant for one of the executives saying to her.

"I'm an employee," she replied, "a member of the Florida Hospital family. I'd like to make an appointment with him to see if he got my appeal."

"He's not available, you can leave a message," came the assistant's curt reply.

"I'd prefer to call back," she said.

"Never leave a message" is another one of the Insurance Warrior's rules. She calls it a felony. Messages get ignored. Call back.

Be a nuisance until they give you what you want: approval. Now Todd has me taking notes so I can improve as an investigative reporter.

Freuler worked the phones all day Monday, until she had made as many calls as necessary to the top executives, urging them to agree to come to contracted rates for her operation.

She went back to work the next day. The call came that afternoon: Her appeal had been approved. She didn't know which decision maker had ruled in her favor. She didn't know how it happened. But it worked.

"That's the stupid part," she said to me. "One person can just flip the switch and say, 'Do it.'" And boom—the appeal is approved.

Freuler's operation went well and though the cancer returned, she has been able to beat it back. Since then she has helped a colleague win an appeal against the health plan to get shoulder surgery. Patients have been conditioned—groomed—by the health care industry, she said. We are told that we have a limited set of options, even if those options aren't what's best for our health. We get steered down a path and told it's the only way to do things. The key to winning an appeal is to do the opposite of what the insurer or health plan says you should do.

Todd summed up her strategy for me in three key principles:

1. **Access is power.** Who you send the appeal to is more important than what you say in the appeal.
2. **Speed is a strategy.** Appeals must always be expedited. If you settle for the standard appeal time—you just lost your appeal.
3. **The phone calls are key.** If you simply deliver your appeal and let them have their way with you—you just lost your

appeal. Take the time to find the personal office phone numbers. The phone calls are your personal access to power.

Todd said she has found that some appeals are not winnable. She doesn't take those. If they don't have science supporting the requested treatment, they won't get any traction with the employer or insurance carrier. And if there is science, it must support a dramatically improved outcome, not a mere reduction in negative symptoms.

Todd also tends to focus only on cases where the stakes are extremely high—like more than $50,000 or life or death for the patient. But she's too busy anyway. She wants you to learn how to do this for yourself and your loved ones. She knows you can follow her lead and do this yourself. You also don't have to wait until your life is at stake or you are facing bankruptcy because of a denial. Making sure your insurance plan covers you will also help you avoid medical debt, which I cover in the following chapter. Use Todd's methods, or a variation on them, anytime your company health plan or insurance company tries to block you from getting the care you need.

Freuler and I closed our conversation by talking about how difficult it sounds to stand up to your insurance company and your employer. Many people will think they don't have the personality type to take on the fight, she said, or that the system is too big, or it's too much of a machine. But if a person's life and financial stability are at stake, they will fight. And maybe they will battle even more, Freuler pointed out, if the life at stake is that of a child or spouse or other loved one. "If you can be that fighter to support and be victorious for a friend or family member—anyone whom you care about—that's a gift more valuable than anything."

TAKE ACTION

The tactics laid out in this chapter may sound overwhelming. But winning an appeal might not be as hard as it sounds, and it's better than losing without a fight. Here's how you start.

1. Buy Laurie Todd's book *Approved: Win Your Insurance Appeal in 5 Days*. Read it. She lays out every step of her process in a way that's easy to follow or adapt to your needs.

2. Know your opponent. Are you in a fully insured health plan? If so, then consult your state insurance department to see which regulations might help with your appeal. Are you in a self-funded plan? Then your employer is setting the terms of the health coverage, so they also need to be targeted with the appeal.

3. Make your case with evidence and social pressure—not emotion. To do medical research, go to Google Scholar and PubMed and look up key words related to your disease or the treatment or medication you need. You can get abstracts of all the scientific literature for free, and those may be enough to make your case. You can also find free versions of many articles online with a little searching. Do not be intimidated by scientific articles. And do not be afraid to reach out to the authors of the articles. Academics and researchers do their work because they care about patients, and they're easy to find online. Send them an email if you have a hard time understanding if their research is helping to make your case. They don't get a lot of calls from the general public and might enjoy hearing from you.

   Go to patient groups online to find people who have had insurers cover the type of care you need. Facebook is an incredible resource here. There are groups for almost any type of medical issue, and if you can't find one, just ask people in any group if they know of a patient group that's focused on the type of issue you need. Then be bold: Tell them your situation and ask them if they've ever heard of an insurer covering the type of thing you need. Patients love to help one another in these types of situations.

4. Speed is a strategy. Work the phones to get decision makers on your side. Identify the key decision makers—for your employer, the insurance company, and any outsiders who could lend an air of gravitas to your case. Email each of them your appeal memo and spend a day calling them all to urge them to approve it or help it get approved.

5. Take a close look at Holly Freuler's appeal, which I've posted on my website, marshallallen.com. It's brilliant and it will show you the layout you want to use. You can make it a model for your appeal.

4

How to Handle Medical Debt Collectors

Y OU MAY BE ONE OF many Americans who lost an insurance appeal and got stuck with huge medical bills. Or maybe you got stuck paying an overpriced bogus bill or hit with an expensive illness like cancer that set you back financially. Perhaps you're among the millions of people who lost your health insurance during the pandemic.

Whatever the circumstances, you might be stuck with medical debt and there might be debt collectors coming after you for payment. If that's the case, you're not alone. The Urban Institute reported in 2019 that about one in six Americans has medical debt in collections. In some counties around the nation almost half the adults have medical debt in collections. If you haven't had a medical debt go to collections, one of your friends almost certainly has. Getting hounded by medical debt collectors is a common problem in our country.

Here's how it works: If a bill goes unpaid for too long, usually around ninety days, your doctor or hospital might call in a debt collector to try to wring the cash out of you. In that case, you still owe the medical provider, but the debt collector also takes a cut of whatever you pay.

If you can't pay your medical bill for three months or six months or a year, your hospital might sell your debt to a debt buyer, just so they can make some money from it. Debt buyers usually pay pennies on the dollar. Old debt is not worth much because there's little hope the patient will ever be able to pay it. Then instead of the hospital's coming after you for payment, you've got the debt buyer's collectors pursuing you for the money.

It's no fun dealing with debt collectors. They may call you from early in the morning to late in the evening. They might tell you that paying off your debt will save your credit, which may or may not be true. You might get threatened with lawsuits or with wage garnishment—having money taken out of your paycheck to cover the debt. Debt collectors aren't supposed to lie to you about all the bad things that could happen if you don't immediately hand them your money, but it happens all too often.

Fortunately, there's hopeful news. With some savvy negotiating it is possible for patients to wipe clean their medical debt for a lot less than they owe. Fear not: The fight isn't over if the debt collectors are bothering you. Your dispute has moved into a new phase that could present fresh opportunities for freedom. In fact, in a dark way your leverage gets better once the debt collectors start calling. They have likely given up on getting everything you owe, so you can negotiate to pay a lot less than the full tab.

One person came to my mind when I thought of the right expert to guide you through this crisis: Jerry Ashton. I had heard many times about Ashton and RIP Medical Debt, the charity he cofounded.[1] He spent decades as a debt collector, but in 2014 he started turning the industry on its head by helping people burdened by debt caused by medical care. RIP Medical Debt purchases and then forgives medical debt, wiping the slate clean for patients—including clearing their credit for the debt that's forgiven.

Ashton sees the medical debt crisis from both sides. He empathizes with the doctors and hospitals that expect payment. He called patients on their behalf for years, which he said he did ethically and with compassion. But he also agrees with the point I've been making in this book: The industry has been so greedy for so many years that it's raised the cost of care beyond what's fair or what patients can bear. "What's been created, by hook or by crook, is not a broken health care system, but a system engineered to reap the most profit possible while still appearing to be patient centered," Ashton said while we sat in his New York City office.

I wanted Ashton to help readers learn what they should do to clear out any medical debt they have in collections. And I also wanted him to help patients learn what they need to do to avoid debt collectors in the first place. I also discuss whether bankruptcy might be the best option to help you and your family, and what to do if you've been sued by a hospital for unpaid medical expenses. There's no magic solution, but Ashton's advice and insights, which I lay out in this chapter, provide a path forward that may come as a surprise. His guidance is a source of hope.

Know who you owe.

To get out from under your medical debt you first need a clear understanding of who owns your debt. There are different types of debt collections. In some cases, you still owe your doctor or hospital or other medical provider. So that's the party telling you to pay up. But if the debt is further along, your medical provider might have *assigned* your bill to a third party, the debt collector, to chase you down for payment. If this is the case, you can still try to negotiate a reduced lump sum or payment plan with the debt collector or perhaps the medical provider. You want to start with the same approach I explained in chapter two, about fighting bogus bills: Find the reasonable price for whatever put you in debt and make sure you didn't get overbilled. But now you also have a valuable piece of information. If your doctor or hospital has enlisted a debt collector, that means they are worried that they're going to get stiffed. They are afraid that you might not pay them anything. Also, the hospital might be thinking about *selling* your debt to a debt buyer. Ashton said he has never heard of doctors selling their debt to a debt buyer, though it could happen in some cases. Since the doctor or hospital is concerned you won't pay the full bill, they may be more open to giving you a massive discount on what you owe. One patient advocate told me when bills are in this phase before they get sold to a debt buyer, she can get a quick pay discount of up to 50 percent.

If the hospital has *sold* your debt, that means they are no longer the party demanding payment. The debt has been purchased and is now owned by a debt buyer, and that entity is now the one pursuing payment. If this is the case, there is no use appealing to the medical provider. They got paid and your debt is out of their hands. It's important to know your debt has been sold because Ashton said it could have been sold for as little as two or three cents on the dollar. Maybe a nickel on the dollar at the most, he estimated. That means the collection agency paid a nickel, at the most, for every dollar that you owe. If your bills total $1,000, the debt buyer just bought them for about $50. That's good to know! The debt buyer doesn't need you to pay the full $1,000, or whatever you owe, to make a profit. He could settle for a fraction of what you owe and still come away with a nice margin. Your goal, Ashton explained, is to persuade him to take something much less than what you owe so he can make his profit and you can be liberated.

Ashton said the discount could be as much as 85 percent, though every situation will vary. So that means if you pay 15 percent of what you owe, the debt buyer will likely get a nice return on his investment and you will get a massive discount that, you hope, you can afford. You might be able to get an even better deal if you pay it off in a lump sum.

So let's say 15 percent is your target. If you owe $1,000, you're going to get them to agree to let you off the hook for $150 or less.

Time to clear the books.

You must dispute the debt in writing within thirty days.

The debt collection industry has been guilty of so much abuse and deception that it's been reined in by a federal law called the Fair Debt Collection Practices Act.[2] The act allows you to dispute a debt, but it must be done in writing within thirty days of being contacted by the debt owner. When you hear for the first time from the entity that purchased your debt, Ashton said you should always dispute the amount they claim you owe. If you fail to dispute the debt in writing within thirty days, the assumption from that point forward is that the debt is legitimate. Do not ignore these collection calls or letters!

I've explained in chapter two how to examine your medical bills to make sure they are accurate and reasonably priced. You may want to follow those steps here. My assumption is your original medical bills were not itemized, so you never did check to see if they were coded properly or priced fairly. And medical bills are so riddled with errors and price gouging that my assumption would be that the entire bill is in dispute, until proven otherwise.

Be sure you send your dispute letter to the debt collector by certified mail so you have a record that they received it. See my sample dispute letter below and adapt it for your dispute.

Make the debt collector verify that they own the debt.

The Fair Debt Collection Act also requires the debt collector to provide the consumer with verification of the debt, and a copy of that verification needs to be sent to the consumer. That's something every patient should demand, Ashton told me. It may be impossible for the debt buyer to produce this information, he said. Many of the debts they pursue are so old, and have been bought and sold so many times, that they can't produce the trail of ownership. The system is that screwed up. In those cases, the debt buyer may throw up their hands and walk away. That doesn't mean the debt is forgiven. If the buyer forgives the debt it may require sending a tax form, Ashton explained, because the IRS considers forgiven debt as income.[3] But asking for verification may make the debt collector go away. It will also signal to them that you're a savvy consumer. That may improve your leverage when you are negotiating with them to pay a much lower price on your debt.

If you want to dispute a debt to a debt collector and demand verification, you must do it in writing. Here's a sample letter Ashton and I adapted from one of the samples provided by the Consumer Financial Protection Bureau:

[Your name]
[Your return address]

[Date]

[Debt collector name]
[Debt collector address]
Re: [Account number for the debt, if you have it]

Dear [Debt collector name],

I am responding to your contact about collecting a debt. You contacted me by [phone/mail], on [date] and identified the debt as [any information they gave you about the debt].

In accordance with the Fair Debt Collection Practices Act, I am writing to inform you that I dispute this debt. I do not believe I owe the amount you are requesting and need you to please waive this debt and clear this account.

If you believe I do owe the debt, in accordance with the Fair Debt Collection Practices Act, I need you to verify that I am responsible for the debt. I also need you to verify that you are the entity that I should pay.

If you have proof of my responsibility for this debt, mail me the documents that you believe verify this as a fact. I also need to see evidence that the prices charged by any medical provider were "usual and customary" amounts the provider would accept from its in-network insurance providers. I need a full accounting. I want to know the date of delivery service, the services delivered, an itemized medical bill, including the original creditor and codes used to document the alleged care provided.

Stop all other communication with me and with this address, and record that I dispute having any obligation for this debt. If you stop your collection of this debt, and forward or return it to another company, please indicate to them that it is disputed. If you report it to a credit bureau (or have already done so), also report that the debt is disputed.

I appreciate your cooperation.

Sincerely,
[Your name]

Simply put: You want the pain and effort you create for the debt collector to be more costly than the rewards they get from pursuing you. It will be labor and time intensive for them to track down the records you are demanding. They will have to put energy into it, and doctors and hospitals are also known for keeping messy records. They might not be able to document that you owe the debt. Even if they continue their pursuit, your demands of them are increasing your leverage if it comes time to negotiate a workable payment for the debt.

You may have other questions or concerns you want to address with your debt collector. For example, maybe the debt isn't yours, and you need to say so. Or perhaps you want to learn more about the debt or tell the debt collector to only contact you through your attorney. If you have these types of concerns, use the other sample letters produced by the Consumer Financial Protection Bureau. All the resources can be found here: https://www.consumerfinance.gov/consumer-tools/debt-collection/.

Each of the bureau's letters will give you an idea for how to frame your letters to debt collectors. You can copy them or revise them to suit your needs.

Let's make a deal.

If you do owe the money, what you really want is for the debt collector to help you wipe the debt clean. You've been dealt a bad hand, but Ashton will help you play it the best you can.

Coming to a payment agreement with a debt collector starts with having the right frame of mind, Ashton explained. You might need to start by getting over any stigma or shame you may feel because of your medical debt. People burdened by medical debt are the victims and walking wounded of our broken and predatory health care system. It's not your fault that our nation's leaders have decided to let profiteers harm you with deceptive practices and price gouging. We spend so much money on health care that every American could have their bills fully covered if our spending was more evenly distributed. But instead we have corporations raking in billions and executives raking in millions a year in salary— while ordinary Americans get sent to collections because they got sick and couldn't pay their bills. It's a moral travesty.

The Consumer Financial Protection Bureau has found this to be true: People who only have medical debt in collections are not like other consumers who haven't been paying their bills. They may have lower credit scores but were less likely to be delinquent on their other bills than other consumers with debt in collections.[4]

Debt collectors may try to use our feelings of shame as leverage, Ashton said. They try to make patients feel like they've done something wrong that led to the debt. Shake it off. If you're suffering from medical debt, it's highly unlikely that you're the one to blame. You or a loved one got sick and needed medical care. Then you got sucked into a predatory industry that's built on deception and price gouging. It's not like you went out and bought a massive TV or took a lavish vacation you could not afford.

You need to come up with the best possible deal for yourself that the debt collector will also find agreeable. Before you get too far with deal making, Ashton had a serious warning: *Do not make a deal with a debt collector that you cannot keep.* If you agree to a payment plan and don't abide by it, missing even one payment, your account goes into default. That means you will owe the entire sum, not the reduced amount. You get one chance to make a deal. Make sure it's one you can afford. "Don't be bullied," Ashton said. "They may want you to agree to a larger monthly payment than what you can handle. Don't give in if you can't afford it."

Your agreement may be to pay a lump sum—and it should be discounted if you pay it all at once. Or you may agree to a payment plan. It's safer to drag out a lot of small payments over time if you're on a tight budget, Ashton said. You can always double up on small payments if you come upon more money. Just make sure there's zero interest, or a low enough interest rate that your debt won't balloon over time.

There isn't a quick and easy fix, but it won't disappear if you ignore it. It also may be impossible to come to an agreement that's doable with your budget. Each patient needs to do the best they can, and they won't know how it will go unless they try.

You may need to consider bankruptcy.

Ashton said people in dire situations should consider bankruptcy. If your assets are worth less than what you owe, he said, it might be a logical step to protect you and your family.

The stigma associated with bankruptcy is misplaced, said Ashton, who said he has gone through it twice in his life. Circumstances are often outside our control, he said, like the COVID-19 pandemic, which caused widespread job loss. "People have this bad feeling that they failed morally if they haven't paid a bill,"

Ashton said. "But the truth is, circumstances happen that put the best and most honorable people under the gun."

It can be expensive to file for bankruptcy, so Ashton recommends people turn to a nonprofit organization called Upsolve.[5] The founder of Upsolve, Rohan Pavuluri, explained to me that his service is like TurboTax for bankruptcy, and the tool is free for people who qualify based on their circumstances and income. "The cruel irony of bankruptcy is that it costs $1,500 in order to tell the court that you have no money," Pavuluri told me. "It's a pervasive civil rights injustice we don't talk about in America."

Pavuluri created Upsolve when he was a student at Harvard University and launched it nationally in 2018. He agreed that Americans need to move beyond the moral stigma attached to bankruptcy. It is a right that has its origins in the U.S. Constitution, he said, and something that's common and accepted in the corporate world. "It helps people after financial shocks that are beyond their control," he said. Most personal bankruptcies are related to medical debt, job loss, or divorce, he said.

A bankruptcy will show up on your credit report for years, but Pavuluri said most Upsolve users already have low credit scores and about $50,000 in debt. Bankruptcy clears the debt and gives them a fresh start, which typically improves their credit rating.

Upsolve is geared for people who have the simplest Chapter 7 bankruptcy cases and who do not own a home or make above the median income in their state, among other considerations. But it also has a listing service to connect anyone who is considering bankruptcy with an independent attorney for a free consultation. The nonprofit organization's revenue comes from donations and fees paid by attorneys who participate in the listing service.

You could bring up bankruptcy when you negotiate with a debt collector. For example, you could tell the debt collector that your financial situation is so bad you might have to file for bankruptcy, in hopes it will lead to a lower payout for your debt.

Love your enemies.

If bankruptcy is not your best option, then Ashton said we must understand and work through the negotiation process by—strangely enough—cooperating with the debt collectors. As we discuss throughout this book, everything is negotiable, and things go smoother when we maintain a good relationship with the people on the other side of the telephone. Ashton said you want to think of it as working together with the debt collector to solve the problem that's in front of both of you. You both have the same goal—to get the debt cleared. Plus, the debt collector may also be one accident or illness away from financial disaster. Who knows—that debt collector may also have medical debt in collections. Take the time to be friendly. Tell them about your kids. Ask them about their family. Explain to them that you're buried in bills and doing the best you can. Ask them if they've ever had a challenge with their finances. Try to get them to explain what their boss wants from them. See if you can learn the minimum amount they can take and still be considered a success when they get evaluated. Getting to know each other can't hurt. It might even make them want to give you a break to the extent that they can.

Ashton compared the way a patient should talk to their medical debt collector with aikido, the martial art that's characterized by redirecting an attack in a peaceful way. His advice made me think of one of the recommendations made by Chris Voss, a former FBI hostage mediator who wrote the best book I've read on negotiating, *Never Split the Difference*. Voss would get called out to the scene when terrorists or bank robbers or other criminals were holding innocent people hostage. He had to persuade the criminals to release the hostages without anybody getting hurt. That took gently poking and prodding the hostage taker like a psychotherapist, to understand their motives and what drove them, so he could persuade them to surrender without causing any bloodshed. To be successful he had to think like they did. He had to empathize with them, to truly understand what made them tick.

Voss said the same principle can apply to any negotiation, and this would include talking to a debt collector. There are parallels because the debt collector is holding your financial future hostage and threatening to do harm to it. You want to calm them down, walk them away from the ledge, and bring them to your side of the table. That means you must think about what's important to them. The worst type of negotiation, Voss explains in his book, is one in which neither side listens to the other. You can't ignore the other side's position because it makes them less likely to do what you want them to do. We need to employ what he calls tactical empathy, which is "the ability to recognize the perspective of a counterpart, and the vocalization of that recognition . . . paying attention to another human being, asking what they are feeling, and making a commitment to understanding their world."[6]

Ashton knows it sounds crazy because people hate debt collectors. But he said when they call you should try to be as pleasant as possible. Don't avoid them and don't hang up on them. Welcome the call and tell them that you'd like to resolve any legitimate bill. "So nice to hear from you today," Ashton said, role playing as if he was responding to a call from a debt collector. "I know you want to help me get this behind me. I can't thank you enough for that. The reality is, however . . ."

I have a favorite line that I like to use whenever I'm negotiating: "I'm sure we will come to an agreement that works well for both of us." I like this phrase because I'm emphasizing that whatever they want also must work for me. But I'm doing it in an agreeable way.

If the debt collector claims you owe $1,000 and your goal is to pay around 15 percent of that total—assuming you can afford to pay that amount—then it's time to talk numbers. The collector is going to come on strong, Ashton warned. They'll say they want the full amount "on their desk by Friday at noon or they will shoot your dog," he said, joking to make his point. The debt collector will start off menacing.

You don't want to counter by saying you will give them $150. You want to build a relationship with them by helping them understand your dire financial situation. Tell them that while you wish you could afford to give them what they're asking for, you're afraid you might not be able to give them anything. But your desire is to find a way to come to an agreement that will work well for both of you. The debt collectors can run a credit report on the people who owe them money, and they have access to data that shows how much money they make, Ashton said. That means it's hard to bluff them. But maybe you can help them see the hardships you face that don't show up on paper, and that might soften their demand for full payment. If you tell them the most you can pay is $150, but you can pay it right now and clear the decks for both of you, Ashton said they might just take it. They can have the fast money "and move on to someone else less brilliant," Ashton said, smiling.

As I mention in other chapters, if your debt is in the thousands of dollars you may also want to bring in a professional patient advocate to help you. You can go to the Advo Connection Directory for referrals, which is online at advoconnection.com, or the National Association of Healthcare Advocacy Consultants, at www.nahac.com. You'll have to pay them but having an expert on your side could help rectify the situation.

Lawsuits and wage garnishment

If your situation has gone from bad to worse, you may have a hospital or debt collector filing a lawsuit to try to recover what they claim you owe. If they win they may try to garnish your paycheck, which means a portion of your pay will be deducted and given to them. Sometimes hospitals even get legal judgments that allow them to go right into the patients' bank accounts and take their money.

Even if this happens, know you're not alone. My friend and collaborator Dr. Marty Makary led a team that published a 2019 study that showed how often hospitals in Virginia garnisheed the wages of their patients.[7] More than a third of the state's hospitals had used the legal system to take money from the paychecks of their patients for unpaid medical debt. More than eight thousand patients had their wages garnished in 2017, the year they studied. Most of them worked for employers like Walmart, Amazon, and Lowe's.

Makary covered this topic extensively in his book *The Price We Pay*, which I had the privilege of editing. I was amazed to see in that book how creative and predatory health care billing can be, and how people can have success when they advocate for themselves.

Makary has started an organization called Restoring Medicine, which is pushing the health care system to become more honest and fair.[8] At many hospitals, their advocacy efforts have shut down the lawsuits being filed against patients.

Hospitals have had an easy path to victory in these lawsuits because patients often don't respond to the case that's filed against them, and then fail to show up for court. Unresponsive and absent patients automatically lose. The patients also almost never have anyone advocating for them. But Makary's experience shows that when a patient is armed with the right information they can win—even in a case where they're being sued.

If you get sued, the next step is similar to what you should do if a debt collector calls: *DO NOT IGNORE THE LAWSUIT.* The worst thing you can do is fail to respond. That will result in a judgment against you for the entire amount of your debt.

Your first step is to try to get an attorney to represent you. The legal world is filled with so many rules and procedures that it's difficult for a nonlawyer to navigate. If you have the money you can hire one yourself. If you don't, try calling your state bar association—the entity that licenses attorneys—to ask for a referral to a legal aid organization in your area. Or Google the name of your city and "volunteer lawyer group" to connect with an attorney who might take your case for free. Many attorneys are required to do a certain amount of free work for clients each year to maintain their license. The volunteer groups are all over the country. If that doesn't work, call your local law school to ask if they have a legal aid clinic that gives their students the opportunity to work on cases for people in the community. These programs are also common.

If you're unable to get an attorney or a law student to help you, dispute the lawsuit yourself. If you don't know how to do that, call the clerk in the court where you're being sued and tell them you need to know the process for disputing the allegations that have been made against you. They can't give you legal advice, but they can at least explain the process and tell you where and when to show up for your case. If you're having trouble getting through on the phone, go to the courthouse in person. The workers in courthouses are accustomed to members of the public looking lost in their hallways. I've been in that situation many times as a reporter and they are incredibly helpful.

To dispute the claim that's being made against you, go through the process I've described earlier in this book to dispute bogus bills and to stand up to debt collectors. Tell them they need to prove that you are indeed the person who owes the debt by providing the paperwork that proves you agreed to pay the debt. You should also ask for them to provide an itemized medical bill that includes the billing codes so you can look up the fair prices for the services. Use the sites HealthcareBluebook.com and FairHealthConsumer .org or hospital websites to check fair prices in your area.

Joseph Kirchgessner, an attorney in Fredericksburg, Virginia, has worked with the Restoring Medicine team to defend about two dozen patients in Virginia. His legal argument—which you could borrow and use in your own defense—is that hospitals require patients to sign what the law calls contracts of adhesion, one-sided agreements that typically involve one party that has a lot of power over another. Courts may void such contracts if there's unequal bargaining power, or if they unfairly require the weaker party to be held to terms they would not have reasonably expected.[9] It's a great argument, but Kirchgessner hasn't even had to make it yet. Every time he steps in to represent a patient, the hospital withdraws its lawsuit. That's a win, for sure, but it doesn't result in the forgiveness of the debt, he said. "We were able to stop one process they used to hurt people," Kirchgessner explained, "but they still want their money."

If you get stuck going to court to face off with a hospital attorney, and you don't have a lawyer to represent you, you could also try asking the judge to appoint a mediator to help you resolve the dispute with the hospital that's suing you. Then you could provide to the mediator your evidence that shows you have been unfairly billed, in the hope the case will be dismissed or that the alleged amount you owe will be reduced. It may be possible to settle the case on the spot for a much lower amount than what the hospital claims you owe.

The final scenario is to try to settle it with the attorney representing the party suing you, Kirchgessner said. Again, if you've done your homework, you might be able to negotiate a much lower settlement than the sticker price.

Ashton and his team at RIP Medical Debt realize that many patients will never be able to negotiate their way out of medical debt. But they need to try. The goal is to minimize the pain as much as possible, Ashton said. And perhaps if people put some of the tactics in this book into use, we can avoid having too many more patients unnecessarily go into debt because of medical care. Ashton recently retired from RIP Medical Debt, but the charity is still working to wipe the debt free on its end. In late 2020, the charity received a $50 million gift from philanthropist MacKenzie Scott that will allow it to expand its work. He said the federal government has also made it easier for hospitals to donate their unpayable accounts to RIP Medical Debt, so they can be easily forgiven. He calls for hospital executives nationwide to donate unpayable accounts so patients can be freed of the burden of debt.

Ashton has now created a new campaign, called Let's Rethink This, which he believes will gain as much traction as RIP Medical Debt. The new venture is encouraging people to stop to rethink the assumptions that have gotten us where we are today—in health care, politics, finance, and more. They might even take a look at why we have so much medical debt. Lurking behind each inspiring story about RIP Medical Debt's work is a darker reality. The charity has bought and forgiven more than $3 billion in medical debt for more than a million families. But the organization is hardly getting started. The medical debt burden carried by Americans is estimated at $1 trillion—and growing.

If you engage debt collectors in a way that's informed and assertive, you can avoid getting sued and also reduce what you have to pay. It's a difficult burden, but by standing up for yourself you can make it a lot lighter, and maybe even be free of it entirely.

In the following chapter I will show how you can turn the tables entirely. You're not the only one who can be sued. I'll show you how it's possible to use small claims court to sue your doctor or hospital or device supplier when they won't play fair with you.

TAKE ACTION

1. Know who you owe. Is it your doctor or a hospital that says you owe money? Or has your debt been sold to a debt collection agency? Your approach to negotiating depends on who you're dealing with.

2. Dispute the debt in writing within thirty days and make the debt collector verify that they own it. Use the letter I adapted from the Consumer Financial Protection Bureau to make your position clear.

3. See all the letters and other resources created by the bureau here: https://www.consumerfinance.gov/consumer-tools/debt-collection/. Copy or revise them to suit your needs.

4. Make a deal. A debt collector might be willing to make a large reduction on what you owe.

5. If you're considering bankruptcy, check out Upsolve.org.

6. Love your enemies. It won't help your negotiations to lose your cool with a debt collector. Try relating to the debt collector like you would a friend. Ask them to come to a reduced payment that works well for both of you.

7. If you're getting sued—do not ignore it. See if you can get an attorney to represent you. Or use the steps described in this chapter to stand up for yourself in court.

5

Sue Them in Small Claims Court

WHEN YOU FIGHT THE health care system it's a David versus Goliath battle. There's an unequal distribution of power. You're the small child with a sling and stones taking on what appears to be an undefeatable giant.

You may not realize it, but our country's judicial system has taken these types of power imbalances into account through its small claims court system.

When you get hit by unfair medical bills, and the doctor or hospital or clinic or insurance company refuses to play fair, you could sue them in small claims court. The lawsuit would be for the amount you're being overcharged. You would need to do your homework, but you wouldn't be stuck talking to some low-level customer service person in a billing department who has no ability to solve the problem. You can, and should, deploy whatever resources you have available to defend yourself against the predatory medical industry. Small claims court might be the most powerful and underused tool at your disposal. You just need to start using it.

You may think this sounds impossible, but don't be intimidated. It's so easy a teenager can do it. I know because, when I was a skinny know-nothing kid, I took on my former employer in small claims court. You could do the same thing.

When I was sixteen, I worked at the Heritage Square Opera House, a dinner theater in Golden, Colorado, where we served guests a sumptuous dinner before they attended a hilarious slapstick Victorian melodrama. I worked in the dining room, carving a giant roast beef. I loved my job.

One day we all showed up for work and they had shut the place down. Even worse, they told us they had no money to pay us what we were owed. That didn't make sense. The opera house had recently opened a new location across town, and that one was still operating. The same person owned it: We knew him as "Bill." If Bill could run his new opera house, then he could pay us. We were young but we weren't dumb.

Bill was none other than G. William Oakley, a legend in Colorado's community theater community. To us, Bill was an intimidating presence. He was heavyset with a beard and glaring eyes and never acknowledged our existence. None of us had ever had the courage to speak to him.

My mom gave me what seemed like the crazy idea to sue him. I was barely old enough to drive, but Mom told me about small claims court, which exists nationwide for powerless citizens to get justice, with no need for attorneys. Maybe I could sue Bill and the opera house to get my money, Mom said. I loved the idea. I and my good buddy who also worked at the opera house filled out the small claims paperwork. I took the time to write the whole story so my argument would be airtight. Bill owed me about $300, so those were my damages—the amount of money I was owed. I had no idea what to expect. But I named Bill as the defendant and paid a small fee to file the case. Then I forgot about it.

A few weeks later, I got a notice in the mail. We had a court date. That alone surprised me. The wheels of justice had been turning behind the scenes. As the date approached, I knew I needed to be ready. I prepped for a Perry Mason moment, when I'd dramatically argue the case in front of the judge.

On the hearing day I was so juiced on adrenaline I could barely breathe. But the hearing was not in a stately courtroom, as I had imagined. It was in a conference room with an administrative judge. When we walked in we were stunned to see, sitting at a table with someone who appeared to be his attorney, none other than Bill himself, in the flesh. I couldn't believe it. I might have been a powerless teenager, but I had harnessed the power of the court to summon The Man.

I got myself psyched for some rhetorical jousting with Bill's attorney, but the reality was low-key. The judge didn't even have us argue our case. He just read my write-up, in which I explained that Bill stiffed us while still operating his other dinner theater. Then he looked at Bill and asked a simple question: "Is this true?"

"Yes," Bill replied.

"Well, then, you need to give these kids their money," the judge told him.

It was over. Simple as that. He didn't even bang a gavel.

My universe stood still as I watched Bill write me a check. Paid in full. He wrote one out to my friend, too, for what he was owed. Incredibly, small claims court had allowed a couple of kids to stand up to a powerful businessman. What a country!

Small claims court allowed a weaker, less powerful, less wealthy person to stand up to injustice—and win.

See what I'm getting at?

You'll have to do your homework, but I've already shown you how to do that throughout this book. Small claims court is not expensive or time consuming, and can force a more powerful person or corporation to play fair.

Fortunately, people are already using small claims court to take on the health care industry. They've given us a road map. And they are showing that it can work. Filing a case in small claims court could work for you. You might not even need to file the case. The mere threat could swing the dispute in your favor. There is a risk: You could lose the case and be ordered to pay the amount you owe. Small claims court elevates the stakes, so that's not to be taken lightly. But if your argument is strong, it's a powerful force for the consumer, and the process is easier than you think.

When the system screws you, fight back.

Alan Levy turned to the courts to help him with his dispute with his insurance plan and medical equipment supplier. Like many Americans, Levy had a high-deductible health plan, which meant that, in addition to his monthly premiums, he had to pay thousands of dollars up front before his insurance plan paid for anything.

I met Levy in his home, which happens to be near where I live in New Jersey.[1] Levy has sleep apnea, a disorder that causes worrisome interruptions in his breathing at night. He showed me his continuous positive airway pressure device, or CPAP, machine. Like millions of people, he relies on the contraption to stream warm air into his nose while he sleeps, keeping his airway open.

Many insurance companies say they cover CPAP machines. But there's often a catch: They require patients to rack up monthly rental fees rather than simply pay for the machine. Patients may have to pay rental fees for a year or longer before meeting the prices insurers set for their CPAPs. But those prices could add up to much more than what a patient would pay on their own. It's bad for any insurance plan to pay more than it should for a medical device. But it's a real outrage for anyone in a plan with a high deductible. And because deductibles reset at the beginning of each year, patients may end up paying much more out of pocket than the machine is worth.

Renting the machine would have cost Levy $104 a month for fifteen months, according to the rules of his insurance plan. So that would be more than $1,500 total. Buying a new machine would have cost him about $500.

Levy's plan required him to reach a $5,000 deductible before his insurance plan paid a dime. So his insurance plan would be requiring him to pay about $1,000 more than the machine was worth.

Levy called the device supplier that worked with his insurer and asked if he could avoid the rental fee and pay $500 up front for the machine, and a company representative said no. That didn't sit right with Levy. "I'm being overcharged simply because I have insurance," Levy protested.

Levy refused to pay the rental fees. He wrote the device supplier a letter disputing the charges: "At no point did I ever agree to enter into a monthly rental subscription." He asked for documentation justifying the cost. The company responded that he was being billed under the provisions of his insurance carrier.

Levy happens to be an attorney and his focus, ironically, is on defending insurance companies in personal injury cases. He didn't waste time arguing with the customer service representatives. He has protected himself about a dozen times by suing companies in small claims court. He said he doesn't try to get out of paying what he owes, but he won't let the companies take advantage of him. Suing in small claims court is like going on offense as a consumer, as opposed to waiting for the medical provider or insurer to send you to collections, which then puts you on defense. You're taking the fight to them instead of letting them bring it to you.

Levy sued the device supplier in the Special Civil Part of the New Jersey Superior Court, which is designated for cases up to $15,000. (Small claims court in New Jersey is for cases involving $3,000 or less in damages. The monetary limits of small claims courts vary, so check for yourself wherever you live.) You don't have to be an attorney to sue in small claims court, or New Jersey's Special Civil Part. So you could take the same approach if you find yourself at a similar impasse.

Levy accused the company of violating the New Jersey Consumer Fraud Act. He had a strong hunch the case would not go to trial. That wasn't his goal. He merely wanted to use the lawsuit as leverage to make the companies treat him fairly. He wanted to create a big enough pain and potential cost for them that they would be fair with him. "I knew they were going to have to spend thousands of dollars on attorney's fees to defend a claim worth hundreds of dollars," he explained to me.

Sure enough, as soon as the device supply company received the lawsuit complaint, the company's attorney called Levy to negotiate. They agreed to allow Levy to pay $600 for the machine. That was higher than retail but better than the more than $1,500 it would have cost to rent the device.

The company declined to speak to me about the case. Levy said that he was happy to abide by the terms of his plan, but that didn't mean the insurance company could charge him an unfair price. "If the machine's worth $500, no matter what the plan says, or the medical device company says, they shouldn't be charging many times that price," he told me. "I don't blame them for playing the system the best they can for their advantage. But when the system screws me, that's when I fight back."

The "open price" contract

You may be able to take Levy's approach in a dispute with a doctor or hospital or insurance company. I loved Levy's story so much I shared it on an episode of *An Arm and a Leg,* an excellent podcast about the high cost of care, created and hosted by Dan Weissmann.[2] Dan is a kindred spirit—using his show to help patients overcome the injustices of the health care system. He put out the call for listeners to provide other examples of defending themselves in court and then dug in on the subject. On one of his later shows he featured two experts who explained the why and the how of patients' suing the medical industry in small claims court.[3] I took notes from the podcast and then called each of them myself to get more details.

Christopher Robertson, professor of law at Boston University, said on the podcast that basic contract law makes some of these outrageous medical bills a "nonproblem" when you fight them legally. When you sign a consent form agreeing to be treated, it doesn't include a price in most cases. That makes it an "open price" contract, Robertson explained. I know this may sound like arcane legal mumbo jumbo, but you can use this tip to bolster your own case. Your signature on your consent form means you have agreed to pay, and the provider agrees to provide the service, Robertson said. But the doctrine of open price contracts does not allow the medical provider to charge just any amount for the service, Robertson said. The law says the price needs to be reasonable.[4]

For the sale of products, in particular, Robertson said this idea of reasonable prices has been codified in the Uniform Commercial Code, the laws governing commercial transactions in the United States. Prices need to be "reasonable" and set in "good faith," according to the code.

Medical providers "can't just make up the charges," Robertson explained to me. "They have to be appropriate ones."

In his book *Exposed: Why Our Health Insurance Is Incomplete and What Can Be Done About It*, Robertson carries the legal argument even further. He said there's a movement of legal scholars who argue that the power health care providers have over patients calls for a more extreme stance by the courts. Patients are vulnerable and powerless when they seek care, and health care providers may have financial reasons for pressing them to undergo treatment. Thus, the courts should take the stance that they must specify a price up front, when it's feasible, or else the price will be presumed to be zero.

Taking a medical provider to small claims court could have risk attached to it, Robertson said. For example, if the judge doesn't think your explanation of reasonable prices makes sense, he or she could rule against you. Then the court proceeding could be used to determine what assets you have in order to pay. Sometimes judges are unfair or biased and don't buy a person's argument, Robertson said. Small claims court is "one of the tools in the toolbox," but may not be what's best for every patient in every situation.

Coming up with a "reasonable" or "appropriate" price is tricky, of course. Hiding the fair prices is the name of the medical industry's game. But, as I mention throughout this book, we can get the billing codes and look to FairHealthConsumer.org and Health careBluebook.com to come up with prices that would be considered reasonable. Also, remember that the federal government now requires hospitals to post on their websites their cash prices and what they get paid by various insurers. Check hospital websites and call other medical providers that perform the same service. We can also use Levy's tactic by finding the cash or retail price of whatever service that's associated with our bill. Sometimes, insured patients pay more with their insurance than they would pay without it. Or we can call other medical providers who provide the same service to ask them what they expect as a fair payment.

The amount you sue for is the difference between the fair price and the high price the medical provider is demanding from you. We aren't trying to get out of paying for health care. We are just demanding a fair price. Most people don't realize they can use the court system so easily to defend themselves against unfair medical bills, Robertson told me. But he agreed that small claims court is extremely effective.

Robertson wrote an online article to help patients learn how to advocate legally for themselves. His blog post highlighted the story of a dad in Los Angeles, Jeffrey Fox—whom I've come to think of as a guerrilla health care fighting hero. Fox's story is so remarkable I had to talk to him about it myself.

Fox laid it out for me. In October 2014 his three-year-old son had a routine checkup with his doctor at UCLA Health, which was in network with his insurance company, meaning his insurer had agreed-upon prices for the services. Fox's wife agreed to the treatment, but no one discussed how much it would cost. As with most health care visits, the family and UCLA Health had entered into an open price contract. The child got referred to a UCLA Health radiology clinic for an ultrasound scan and Doppler procedure. The scans took about fifteen minutes.

UCLA Health billed him $2,448, which included what was owed for the hospital and the doctors' fees. The insurance company discounted the bill to $1,992, and paid UCLA Health a mere $293. The radiologist billed a separate fee, which Fox paid. That left him with a balance of $1,444.

When Fox opened the bill, he knew he wasn't going to pay it. Healthcare Bluebook showed a total fair price estimate of $518 for the same thing. UCLA Health didn't know it, but Fox was no pushover. He started working in his dad's law office when he was thirteen and said he's sued companies about ten times in small claims court, with success every time. "I love suing businesses," he told me. "Usually when I file, they call up and ask to settle."

Fox did a detailed write-up of his case, which I've included in Appendix A of this book. Check it out because the way he fought the case can be replicated. I will summarize it here. He said he started by calling UCLA and telling them the charges were not reasonable for a fifteen-minute procedure. He didn't get anywhere on the phone, so in December 2014 he sent a letter disputing the charges as invalid, because they had no mutual agreement on the price before the procedure. UCLA's failure to provide a price implies it intended to charge something reasonable, he wrote.

UCLA rejected his argument and said he still owed the money. Fox was getting notices saying that he might be sent to collections and he feared his credit would be damaged by the unpaid bill. That's when he came up with an innovative strategy. In February 2015 he drove down to the UCLA billing office and asked for the manager, whom he knew by name from his previous phone calls.

"Hi, I'm Jeffrey Fox," he said, recalling the conversation to me. "I'd like to pay my bill."

The manager had a look of satisfaction on his face as Fox paid the $1,444 with his credit card. Fox got a receipt, showing the account was paid in full, as the manager looked to send him along on his way.

"And now I have something for you," Fox told the manager. He handed the billing manager a letter that said: "This is a demand that you pay me $1,444.37, which represents the amount that you overcharged me . . ." If you decide to pay the disputed amount and then sue for the refund, Robertson said it's extremely important to document that you disputed the payment. He said you should write "Payment under protest" in the memo line on the check. That way no one can later argue in court that you were not disputing it. "You have to show you had a continuous dispute even during the payment," he said.

In Fox's case, in his refund demand it said to refund the money in fifteen days, or "I will sue you in small claims court." "When I prevail, you will have to pay the amount requested, plus court costs."

"When I prevail." . . . Ohhhhh, I like it. That's the mix of strategic thinking and moxie we all need to have when we stand up to these bullies. The health care system bills like a kid playing checkers. Fox plays chess.

Fox asked the manager to please sign his copy of his demand letter so he had a confirmation that he had received it. The manager refused, turned red in the face, and stormed out of the room.

UCLA Health didn't comply with Fox's demand for a refund. So he filed his case against the Regents of the University of California on March 19, 2015. He wrote a narrative of the case that said Healthcare Bluebook showed a $518 fair price estimate.

The trial date came around about two months later, and he brought his written correspondence with UCLA and a printout of the Bluebook estimate. But no one from UCLA Health showed up. So Fox won a judgment for $1,474, his damages, plus court costs. Talk about flipping the script. Now UCLA Health owed him money!

Your legal threat might bend them to your will.

We should consider Lisa Berry Blackstock as another one of our field generals who guide our battle plan. She launched an estate services company in 1990 that morphed into a patient advocacy business she calls Soul Sherpa.[5] She has used the small claims court tactic a couple of hundred times and it's become a go-to solution when medical providers won't give her client a fair price.

Blackstock said she can't keep up with the desperate phone calls she gets from patients and their loved ones. But people often don't need to hire a professional patient advocate, she told me. If they make the right moves and follow her step-by-step process, they can leverage the medical billers into giving them a price that's fair. If the dispute escalates to a point where the medical provider won't play fair, then legal action by the patient is an excellent option, she told me.

"If you approach the right people, the right way, there is no rulebook," Blackstock said. "You can make your own."

Here is the approach Blackstock takes to resolve an unfair medical bill.

The first several steps involve the same ground we have already covered in this book. You want to get your medical records and an itemized medical bill, with billing codes, and identify any errors on the bill or the way your insurance plan paid the bill. Then compare the prices you've been charged with what others might pay, by calling other facilities and asking for the cash price and looking at the HealthcareBluebook.com and FairHealthConsumer.org websites. You can also check the hospital websites, as I've mentioned, for the Medicare and cash prices, and prices paid by other insurance companies.

Blackstock said you want to come up with the usual, customary, and reasonable price. I've referred to it elsewhere in this book. When we use the UCR, we signal to the industry that we know what we're talking about, which hopefully will make them treat us fairly.

Here's where Blackstock's advice is uniquely suited to filing a case in small claims court. Once you've done those initial steps and established your usual and customary price, write a letter to whoever is sending you the bill, notifying them of your intent to sue them in small claims court if they will not comply with what is fair. Blackstock says don't even bother calling on the phone because the customer service people typically don't have the authority to make changes for you. She said they also often don't know what they're talking about. They give customer service people a script and tell them not to veer from it, she said. Plus, putting it in writing creates the paper trail you may need later in court. In your letter, cite the sources of your information. For example, say, "I looked at the website FairHealthConsumer.org and it says the usual and customary price for this procedure is $XXX. . . ." The fair price that you found is the most you're going to offer for the services you received. Send the letter via certified mail—again, so you have a record that you can refer to in court—to the billing department and, if possible, also the general counsel's office for whatever entity you intend to sue. Warn them in the letter that your intent is to sue them in small claims court if they do not adjust the price to an amount that is fair for both of you. I included one of Blackstock's letters in Appendix B so you can adapt it for your situation.

Typically, the letter alone is enough to make the biller reduce the price, you hope to the amount that's fair, Blackstock said. None of these entities wants to pay their attorney hundreds of dollars an hour to hassle with fighting with you. It's much easier—and cheaper—for them to come to the table to negotiate in a way that's fair.

But if your offer isn't accepted, then you have evidence to attach to your small claims complaint. You will be able to show the court that you did everything you could to resolve the dispute in a way that was fair and that your opponent refused to comply. You will also demonstrate that you've done your homework to show what's fair and how you're being mistreated. That will help your case.

If all else has failed, you are now well positioned to file your case. Small claims courts have varying limits and costs. As I mentioned, in New Jersey, where I live, the small claims limit is $3,000 and it costs $35 to file a case. New Jersey also has the Special Civil Part that allows for cases up to $15,000. In Colorado, where I grew up, the limit is $7,500. If the amount in dispute is higher than the limits, you may not be able to file your case. Or you may be able to sue for the limit set by the court, but forgo the right to pursue anything above the limit. Each court has its own rules and limits, and the information is easy to find online.

Blackstock said her method works every time, and she almost never has to take them to court.

Fox said each small claims court produces brochures and guides that explain the process. He said it's essential to follow the rules carefully: Name the defendant properly, serve the defendant, get proof of the service to the court, and more. Court clerks can't give legal advice but are extremely helpful whenever I need questions answered for a story I'm covering. Check with the clerks to make sure you are following all the procedures properly.

Don't go easy when it's time to collect.

Once you obtain a judgment in court, it's time to collect if the medical provider owes you money. A judgment is a legal order, but sometimes the defendants don't pay up. Fox said he had to use some muscle to get his refund from UCLA Health, which didn't initially pay him his money. The guide produced by the California court system explains that a debtor can be forced to provide a statement of assets. Then you can ask the sheriff to take those assets from the debtor so you can get paid. Fox liked this idea, so he said he threatened UCLA Health, saying if it didn't refund his money, he would have sheriff's deputies come to confiscate their computers and sell them at auction. He told me he used a little imagination to come up with the threat, because he didn't know if that was exactly how such a thing would take place. But it worked. UCLA sent him a check via FedEx.

The deputies may have never come running in response to Fox's demand for payment. But a patient suing a medical provider for an unfair bill and then threatening to call in law enforcement to get paid is a stylish flourish. Thus, Fox's name became legendary in the lore of fighting the predatory nature of the American health care system.

TAKE ACTION

1. Identify your damages—what you feel you are owed. You can do this by getting an itemized medical bill and checking the billing codes against the prices on Healthcare Bluebook.com or FairHealthConsumer.org. You can also call medical facilities and check hospital websites to get the cash, Medicare, and other insurance company prices for different procedures.

2. Look up your local small claims court to see how you would file a case. Just Google "small claims court" and your location to find it. Make sure your damages fall within the limits for small claims court, which will differ from place to place.

3. Send a demand letter to the doctor or hospital or whoever it is that is the source of your dispute. Make your demand to them for whatever you consider to be a fair resolution and warn them that if they do not comply you will be suing them in small claims court on a specific date within fifteen or twenty days of the receipt of your

letter. Send the letter via certified mail so there's a record of its arrival. And send it to the billing department and to the general counsel or whichever attorney is representing the party that's causing the dispute. Use the sample letter in Appendix B that was provided by Blackstock.

4. Be willing to negotiate a settlement outside of court if they are willing to do so.

5. Show up in court to argue your case, using your research to support your argument.

6. Collect! If you win the case and your opponent isn't paying up, check the court to see what resources it has to pressure people to pay up.

Section one of this book focused on what you need to do to fight back against bogus medical bills, your insurance plan, debt collectors, and more. I showed how your fight may culminate with you protecting yourself by filing a suit in small claims court.

You probably noticed that the action steps are often related. They also build upon one another and enable you to gather the information you need for each phase of your fight. Here I can sum up many of the steps:

1. Obtain a copy of all relevant medical records.

2. Obtain an itemized bill that shows each of the charges with its corresponding medical billing code.

3. Make sure the bills accurately reflect the care that was provided to the patient. Dispute any errors.

4. Check the prices that the medical providers charged for the services you received. Use the sites HealthcareBlue book.com and FairHealthConsumer.org and call the same people sending you the bills and others to ask for the cash price for the same services. The federal government requires hospitals to post their prices online for many common procedures, so check their websites. If they aren't posting prices, demand that they do. Push back if any of the charges on your bill are higher than what you are seeing elsewhere in your community.

5. If you have insurance coverage, make sure your plan paid the bills properly. Contest any problems you see.

6. Get help from other patients through online groups or consult a patient advocate.

7. If necessary and possible, sue them in small claims court. The court system exists to address inequities like these. Our taxes fund it. You may be able to use the information you've gathered to argue a compelling case and come out victorious.

We have been conditioned to be passive and to trust our health care system to treat us fairly. But often that doesn't happen. You literally cannot afford to stand back and get steamrolled by a profit-driven system that isn't focused on what's best for patients. The action steps I've provided will vary depending on the situation, but the mindset will not. I can't wait to hear from you when you share your victory stories with me. Each one is yet another example that you can win these battles. And even if the battle does not come out in your favor, you will have maintained your dignity by standing up for what's right.

PART II

Avoiding the Need to Fight

PART ONE OF THIS BOOK FOCUSED ON HELPING YOU WORK through any urgent needs you might be facing, like bogus bills or an insurance company denial. Many of you are facing a crisis *right now*, so I wanted to hit those topics first.

But let's say you haven't been hit with a ridiculously overpriced, error-laden medical bill. The best thing to do is avoid the problem in the first place. Once you've undergone a service or medical treatment, the bill will be on its way. There's little forgiveness. Whenever possible, our best tactic is to steer clear of the problems before they occur. I'm reminded of the ancient wisdom of Sun Tzu, the Chinese general, military strategist, and philosopher who wrote *The Art of War*, the famous book on military strategy. "The greatest victory is that which requires no battle," he wrote.

The following three chapters will show you how to win the battle by avoiding it altogether. Putting these principles into practice before you undergo medical care could save you hundreds or thousands of dollars without giving up any of the high-quality medical care that you and your loved ones need.

6

How to Avoid Treatment You Don't Need

WHEN THE COVID-19 PANDEMIC forced the temporary cancellation of all elective operations in hospitals across the country it caused them to crater financially. Facilities make some of their best profit margins on elective operations.

But some experts pointed to a silver lining.[1] It's likely that many patients were protected from undergoing care that they *didn't need* and then paying for it.

The American epidemic of unnecessary medical treatment is one of the reasons your health care costs keep going up. Experts estimate it's wasting hundreds of billions of dollars a year. That's not some number that's detached from you and me. We pay higher monthly insurance premiums and larger deductibles because of all this care the system is providing that people don't need. Examples are all around us. Many women still get annual cervical cancer testing when it's recommended for every three to five years.[2]

Healthy patients are often subjected to a battery of unnecessary lab work before elective operations.[3] Surgeons perform spine operations when some patients might be better off with physical therapy.[4]

What are you supposed to do about unnecessary medical care? Well, sometimes there's nothing you *can* do about it. If you're undergoing emergency treatment or something urgent there may not be time to check to make sure everything they're doing is necessary. But that's not true in most cases. Thus, any strategy to protect your paycheck and pocketbook needs to address how your money gets thrown away on things you don't need. Every medical procedure or drug comes with physical risks, especially when it's unnecessary. And it all comes at a cost—we waste money and contribute to higher medical costs for ourselves and others.

In this chapter you'll learn about the extent of the unnecessary health care treatment and how to avoid it yourself. I will share the key questions you can consider and pass along to your doctor to ensure that you don't undergo treatment you may not need.

The health care system wastes obscene amounts of money—and it's costing you.

It's rare for anyone to try to tally the precise cost of unnecessary care. But when they do, the estimates are staggering. The Washington Health Alliance, a nonprofit dedicated to making care safe and affordable, analyzed insurance claims from 1.3 million patients who received one of 47 tests or services that are considered overused or unnecessary. What they found should make patients and doctors rethink that next referral. In a single year more than 600,000 patients underwent a treatment they didn't need, costing an estimated $282 million. More than a third of the money spent on the health care services went to unnecessary care, their study found.[5]

Unnecessary medical care has "become so normalized that I don't think people in the system see it," Dr. Vikas Saini told me. Saini is president of the Lown Institute, a Boston think tank focused on making health care more effective, affordable, and just. Lown researchers have shown how overtreatment happens across the spectrum of medical care. Doctors may push for cesarean sections for their own convenience, not so moms and babies can be healthy. Breast cancer, prostate cancer, and thyroid cancer get overdiagnosed, leading to harmful and costly treatment. Around a third of colonoscopies are unnecessary, research has shown. That's not just wasting our money. It's also putting us at risk of harm.

Many studies highlight factors that contribute to the problem. Doctors who take money from pharmaceutical companies are more likely to prescribe the pricey brand-name drugs manufactured by those same companies.[6] Research has also shown that doctors who purchase magnetic resonance imaging (MRI) machines ordered substantially more MRIs for their patients.[7]

Saini and his research colleagues put it bluntly: "Physicians routinely act in conformity with their financial interests."[8]

Saini also pointed out that the whole industry is pushing clinicians to do more, whether or not the patient needs the treatment. "Providers are getting constant messages from superiors or partners to maximize revenue," he said. "In this system we have, that's not a crime. That's business as usual."

This has been going on for so long because patients can hardly push back. They have a hard time shopping for care and often don't have control over the care they receive, Saini said. The medical evidence may support multiple paths for providing care, but patients are unable to tell what is or is not discretionary, he said. Time pressure adds urgency, which makes it difficult to discuss or research various options. "It's sort of this perfect storm where no one is really evil but the net effect is predatory," Saini said.

Another surgeon used a different saying to describe the motives behind overtreatment: "Doctors eat what they kill." In other words, they get paid a fee for performing an operation or doing treatment or seeing more patients. No action, no payment. The industry makes its money by doing stuff—whether or not you and I need it.

In other words, doctors are just like the rest of us. If my publisher paid me a dollar a word for this book, trust me, you'd be getting "overtreated," too. I would be tempted to write a million words!

It's hard to question your doctors when they are pressing a course of treatment. But these are conversations you should be demanding. You are the customer, so you have every right to assert yourself. Plus, you will get stuck with the bill, and it's likely to be overpriced. That means your time for action is now. You must prepare in advance so you can ask the right questions. Here are some of the key questions you can ask to avoid unnecessary care.

KEY QUESTION: Is this procedure or medication or treatment actually necessary?

Unnecessary care can happen when you least expect it. One of the craziest examples I ever documented was the case of a mom who brought her five-year-old daughter to Children's Hospital Colorado because the band of tissue that connected her tongue to the floor of her mouth was too tight. The condition, literally called being tongue-tied, made it hard for the girl to make "th" sounds. It's a common problem with a simple fix: an outpatient procedure to snip the tissue.

During a preoperative visit, the mom said the surgeon offered to throw in a surprising perk. Should we pierce her ears while she's under?

It seemed like an odd request, but the mom agreed, assuming it would be free.

Her daughter emerged from surgery with her tongue newly freed and a pair of small gold stars in her ears. Only months later did the mom discover her cost for this add-on: $1,877.86 for "operating room services" related to the ear piercing. Her insurance company refused to pay the fee, reasonably, because it wasn't medically necessary.[9]

At first, the mom assumed the bill was a mistake. She complained in phone calls and in writing, but the hospital wouldn't budge, and even threatened to send her to collections.

Using operating room time to pierce a girl's ears doesn't happen every day, but the case of the overpriced ear piercing points to the bigger issue.

Too often, it's our children who are subject to unnecessary medical care. Researchers from the University of Michigan looked at data for 8.6 million children in a dozen states to see how often they received care that experts have determined has little value. They scoured the data for certain diagnostic or imaging tests, prescription drugs, unnecessary vitamin D screening, imaging for acute sinus infections, antibiotics for colds, and more. They found that about 10 percent of children received unnecessary services at least once in 2014 and about 3 percent had it happen at least twice.[10] Parents and doctors tend to believe prescribing a drug or ordering a test is better than nothing, "even though the right answer is often to do less," one of the researchers said in a statement about the study. Doctors may also order some type of treatment for fear of missing a problem, the researcher said.

Once you've undergone medical care—necessary or not—you get ushered into the morass of bogus medical billing and collections I mentioned in part one of this book. The mother in the ear piercing story found this out the hard way.

After I contacted the hospital to inquire about the pricey piercing the facility sent the mom a letter saying that "the remaining balance of $1,877.86" would be removed "as a one-time courtesy adjustment."

That's not uncommon. When journalists start calling doctors and hospitals on behalf of patients, the medical providers scurry. They want to get out ahead of the story so that they don't look like the bad guys even though it was their stonewalling of the patient that led the reporter to get involved. Sadly, the stakeholders in the health care industry often seem to care a lot more about their reputation than they do about how they treat people in the first place.

The self-pay manager at the hospital added that they hadn't done anything wrong. The account was "correctly documented, coded, charged and billed according to industry standards," she wrote.

And that's just the problem. The hospital's $1,877 bill for the ear piercing *was* within industry standards. The health care industry makes hundreds of billions of dollars a year providing unnecessary treatment and then making us pay for it. That's the industry standard, but it doesn't mean it's right.

The mother and daughter had to endure one additional insult. The surgeon's piercing was off center on one ear. This time they did it at the mall for about thirty bucks.

KEY QUESTION: Is there a simpler or less expensive option available?

You may find yourself feeling pressured to undergo some type of test or treatment. If so, it may be better to wait, if you can. Christina Arenas might have saved herself a lot of pain and expense and hassle if she had waited instead of giving in to the treatment being pushed on her. Arenas is a young woman who has a history of noncancerous cysts in her breasts. A few years ago, when she was thirty-two, her gynecologist found some lumps in her breast and sent her for an ultrasound to rule out cancer. She wasn't worried. But on the day of the scan, the sonographer started the ultrasound, then stopped to consult a radiologist. They told her she needed a mammogram before the ultrasound could be done.

Overtreatment related to mammograms is a common problem. The national cost of false-positive tests and overdiagnosed breast cancer is estimated at $4 billion a year, according to a 2015 study in *Health Affairs*.[11] Some of this is fueled by anxious patients, some by doctors who fear that missing a cancer diagnosis can be grounds for a medical malpractice lawsuit. But advocates, patients, and even some doctors note the screenings can also be a cash cow for physicians and hospitals.

Arenas, an attorney who is married to a doctor, told them she didn't want a mammogram. She didn't want to be exposed to the radiation or pay for the procedure. But sitting on the table in a hospital gown, she felt like she didn't have much leverage to negotiate.

So she agreed to a mammogram, followed by an ultrasound. The findings: no cancer. As Arenas suspected, she had cysts, fluid-filled sacs that can afflict women her age. The radiologist told her to come back in two weeks so they could drain the cysts with a needle, guided by yet another ultrasound. But when she returned, she got two ultrasounds: one before the procedure and another as part of it.

The radiologist then sent the fluid from the cysts to pathology to test it for cancer. That test confirmed—again—that there wasn't any cancer. Her insurance whittled the bills down to $2,361, most of which she had to pay herself because of the high-deductible design of her insurance plan.

Arenas told me she didn't like paying for something she didn't think she needed and resented the loss of control. The law requires patients to provide their consent with any treatment. So when doctors pressure you to do something you don't want to do without presenting other reasonable options, it may be a violation of your rights. It didn't feel right to Arenas. "It was just kind of 'Take it or leave it.' The whole thing. You had no choice as to your own care."

Arenas's doctors at the large Washington, D.C., doctor group that provided her treatment declined to speak to me. In her medical records they're shown saying that they think the care was appropriate.

With Arenas's permission, I shared her case with experts, including Dr. Barbara Levy, vice president of health policy for the American College of Obstetricians and Gynecologists, and three radiologists. All of them agreed that at least some amount of overtreatment took place. Doctors often choose to order imaging tests rather than drain apparent cysts, Levy said. "We're so afraid the next one might be cancer even though the last ten weren't," she said. "So, we overtest."[12]

Arenas knew she'd been given care she didn't need. She discussed it with one of her husband's friends who is a gynecologist. She learned the process could have been much simpler and more affordable. She could have had her cysts drained without images in her gynecologist's office for about $350, which is what she does now.

On a couple of occasions Arenas said she's even gone to extreme measures—using a needle at home to drain the cyst herself. She said it was more convenient to do it that way and at the time she was worried she would be subjected to more unnecessary tests.

Again, the overtreatment led to a battle over the bills. Arenas complained, but the medical group denied her request to reduce the amount owed. Then bill collectors got involved, so she threatened legal action. She said she never got to speak to anyone. Her demand was routed to an attorney, who declined her request because there was "no inappropriate care." She also complained to her insurance company and the Washington, D.C., attorney general's office, but they declined to help reduce the bill.

Arenas ended up paying the bill and said it's led to some valuable lessons that you could also apply to your future visits with doctors. **If you feel you're being coerced into a treatment, you can refuse it.** Assuming it's not an emergency, you could call your prescribing doctor or another physician to ask about the best course of action. "Get a second opinion or get your service performed somewhere else," Arenas said.

You could ask for a breakdown of the potential cost for the recommended treatments. "Don't assume because the procedure is simple, the cost will be low," Arenas said. This is a crucial point, because once you've undergone treatment you can't control what they demand that you pay. If the doctors don't know the cost, as they often don't, the information should be available from the facility's patient advocacy department. Just keep in mind that any patient advocates whose paychecks are coming from the medical institution are not really on your side. But they could help you get the information you need, like the price of a procedure or test. Also, now that hospitals are required by the federal government to post their prices online there should be no excuse for not telling patients what various services will cost.

So what are we supposed to take from all of this? I'm reminded of another self-defense saying: "Survive to fight another day." In many cases we do not have to have the care provided right at that time, on that day. If we feel like we're being pressured into treatment it might be best to walk away—if that's possible—and see what some other experts think.

KEY QUESTION: What does the United States Preventive Services Task Force recommend?

You might feel intimidated asking your doctor questions. Physicians are obviously supersmart and have trained for years to establish their expertise. Too often it's like they're running you through an assembly line, so you don't feel like you have a chance to slow things down with a question. And sometimes they act sanctimonious, talking as if the medical industry is all evidence based. But that's often not the way it happens on the front lines. It's sadly common for a doctor's recommendations to go against the best science.

So how can you know? In some cases you can turn to the advice of the United States Preventive Services Task Force. It's an independent group of volunteer experts who examine the most current research on medical treatment and then establish guidelines.[13] Unlike most medical advocacy groups, many that also make recommendations, the task force does not take industry money. It's funded by our taxes. And each member discloses any potential conflicts of interest.[14] The task force pores over the latest and best research on important treatment topics and establishes guidelines about the best path forward for patients. It has more than one hundred published guidelines on the most common types of screening and the use of medication that is supposed to prevent problems.

My wife recently had her doctor making recommendations that came into conflict with the task force's guidance. At the time, my wife was forty-eight and healthy and at low risk of breast cancer. Her ob-gyn checked her breasts for lumps—thankfully, there were no concerns—and then promptly gave her a prescription for a mammogram. That sounds sensible—my wife's doctors have been telling her every year for the past decade to get a mammogram. And the doctors have good reason. They're trying to catch any hint of breast cancer early. They want to protect their patients.

But if you take an independent look at the evidence, a mammogram was not necessarily the best course of treatment for my wife. Mammograms frequently lead to false positives that create panic and unnecessary treatment—harmful and expensive breast biopsies and even lumpectomies and radiation treatment. This doesn't mean mammograms aren't vital in many cases, but they are not appropriate in all cases.

The task force publishes guidelines about using a mammogram to screen a healthy woman for breast cancer. If a woman is under fifty, it does not recommend the test. "There is at least moderate certainty that the net benefit is small," the guideline says.[15] Of course, the task force also says that the decision to get a mammogram is an individual one.

There are other guidelines that say women in their forties should get routine mammograms, but they come from groups that are funded by the medical industry or whose members may profit from mammograms.[16] Whenever we consider recommendations we should also look at who is funding the organizations producing the guidance. Money and financial conflicts of interest often sway what becomes shared with us as science- or evidence-based medicine.

When my wife decides whether to get a mammogram, she talks it over with me and gives more weight to the guidelines that are established by independent medical experts, not the ones created by people who may have financial conflicts of interest. Her decision is based on the best evidence and science. But when she told her ob-gyn she didn't want the mammogram, the doctor didn't discuss the evidence. Instead, she gave her the stink eye and used social pressure to push for the mammogram. "Every other doctor and basically everyone in the medical industry would disagree and say you need a mammogram at age forty," the ob-gyn told my wife.

That's an astonishing response when you consider it flies in the face of the best—by "best" I mean science-based and "independent"—medical evidence we have in this country. But brace yourself because this reaction is common when the industry is on autopilot, churning through appointments and pressing forward with more and more treatment, whether or not it's medically justified.

Be ready for similar pushback if you ask your physician questions. You may want to bring a friend or family member with you to an appointment, if you're nervous or unable to focus or somehow incapacitated. You may even want to cite the task force's guidance and ask the doctor to consider how their recommendations adhere to what independent experts suggest.

KEY QUESTION: What are the chances that this treatment will work? What are the risks?

One of our problems as Americans is that we've been conditioned to think that doing something is always better than not doing something. And the medical industry is right there with us because it makes more money when we do more. Recently, some of my best friends asked me if I could help a good friend of theirs find a back surgeon. I had met Jeff previously and he's in his forties and in great shape. He's a third-degree black belt in tae kwon do—an accomplished martial artist. But he'd been having intense neck pain caused by herniated disks and was considering surgery. Jeff wanted me to help him find the best surgeon for his procedure. That's something I do a lot for my friends, but in Jeff's case I knew he needed to think through some more fundamental questions. Back and neck pain is incredibly common and spinal surgery is often not the answer. The operations often don't work.[17] And spine surgery also comes with risk: infections, paralysis, loss of flexibility, and more. A study in the *Annals of Internal Medicine* compared the outcomes of patients who underwent lumbar spine surgery with those who did physical therapy. Two years later the study found no difference in pain or physical function between the two groups. Plus, about a fourth of the patients in the surgery group suffered complications, such as repeat surgery or an infection from the operation, while about 10 percent of the physical therapy group felt worsening symptoms.[18]

Remember when you consult surgeons: They typically get paid when they operate. It's likely that one of their incentives is to put you under the knife.

Studies show that patients considering spinal surgery should try other types of care first, like physical therapy, before they have a surgeon slice into their bodies. They should take their time, if possible, to get multiple opinions from surgeons and other doctors and providers, such as physical therapists and chiropractors, to make sure surgery is the only reasonable option. This is true for other types of treatment, too. Your doctor may recommend it, but do you really need to get an MRI scan? Maybe a different scan would be better. Or perhaps you had one recently, so it doesn't need to be duplicated. Your doctor may recommend a brand-name drug, but there may be a generic equivalent that is just as good— the same chemical makeup—for a much lower price.

Jeff consulted a neurosurgeon who told him he needed an operation right away. Another surgeon also said he was a candidate for surgery. But Jeff didn't feel like he should rush into the operation and it turns out he didn't need surgery. He went on a Keto diet—increasing healthy fats and reducing carbohydrates, with intermittent fasting. He also did half a dozen sessions of physical therapy, along with exercises at home. He has continued to lift weights and exercise, but also backed off on the type of training that could irritate his neck.

I saw Jeff months later and he told me the problems had been resolved, without surgery. All in all, he has felt fine because of the physical therapy and lifestyle changes. He shook his head when he thought about how his surgeons had been steering him toward the operating room.

KEY QUESTION: What happens if we wait?

Start by asking this key question next time you or a loved one is weighing some type of elective or discretionary service or test or procedure: "What's the worst thing that could happen if we wait?" It's a dumb question if you're in the middle of an emergency because the answer will be obvious. But in many cases a doctor has recommended a particular drug or treatment and we are trying to decide. Asking "What happens if we wait?" may be the most important question to protect us from a host of financial and physical problems. It crystalizes the conversation in a way that can help us avoid something we don't need. It requires a doctor to lay out the risk of *not taking action* so we can compare it with the *risk of taking action*.

None of the questions in this chapter should cause you and your loved ones to avoid getting the treatment you need. But each of them can protect you from getting medical treatment you don't need. Avoiding unnecessary care won't just protect your bank account. It may also protect you from additional health problems caused by medical errors or complications related to medical care. Medical mishaps are one of the leading causes of death in the United States.[19]

And if you're certain that you need a particular type of test or treatment, the following chapter will make sure you find the care you need for the best price.

TAKE ACTION

1. I included some of the Choosing Wisely campaign's five key questions in this chapter. Ask them to make sure you receive the tests, treatment, and procedures you need—and avoid the ones you don't.[20]

    i. Do you really need this test or procedure or medication? Ask how what's being recommended will specifically address what's ailing you or your loved one.

    ii. What are the risks? All drugs and treatment have possible side effects. What are they? What are the chances that test results will be inaccurate or inconclusive? Could those results lead to more testing or another procedure? Project the treatment plan forward to see how certain it is to lead you where you want to go.

    iii. Are there simpler, safer options? Sometimes the treatment is more dangerous than the disease. Or something like changes to your lifestyle or eating habits or exercise can have the same effect.

    iv. What happens if you don't do anything? Will your condition get worse—or possibly better—if you don't do anything right away?

    v. How much does it cost? Often there are less expensive tests or treatments. Sometimes the treatment is cheaper if you don't use insurance, so check the cash price. See if there are generic drugs instead of brand-name medications.

2. Consult the recommendations of the U.S. Preventive Services Task Force next time you are considering some type

of medical treatment: https://www.uspreventiveservices taskforce.org/uspstf/. The National Institute for Health and Care Excellence, known as NICE, performs a similar function in England: https://www.nice.org.uk/.

3. Get a second opinion before agreeing to any costly or invasive treatment, or any medication.

4. Ask your doctor or medical practitioner what I consider to be the single most important question before undergoing any treatment or test or agreeing to take any medication: "What happens, or what are the risks, if we wait?"

7

Protect Yourself from Price Gouging

A COUPLE OF YEARS AGO I had the most remarkable health care experience of my life. My wife has suffered with headaches since she was a little girl, and on this day her migraine had become so intense and persistent she was in tears. She needed a doctor to check her out and prescribe some powerful pain medication.

These things never seem to happen when it's convenient. It was after hours. We couldn't hit up the budget-friendly options, like a doctor's office or urgent care. The hospital was our only choice. Her hands cradled her head as we shuffled through the doors of the emergency room. But I was wincing, too. These ER bills were about to give both of us a headache.

I steadied myself as we approached the front desk. Every new doctor my wife sees for her headaches is tempted to do a full workup, including pricey brain scans, whether or not she needs it.

I also know how common it is for ER doctors to not have contracted rates with insurance plans. I pictured a surprise medical bill for thousands of dollars coming in the mail weeks later from the physician. Her sickness and the urgency of our situation made us ripe for the industry's exploitation. Easy pickings. The doctors and hospital could hit us with almost any price, and we'd have to pay it.

I was practically ready for combat when I walked in the door, but to my surprise, the clerk didn't even ask about my insurance plan. He told me I could pay cash. I was about to ask the dreaded question: "How much?" But he was already clicking keys on his computer. My eyebrows rose as he printed what appeared to be—gasp—an invoice. It described the charge as a "consultation fee" and the amount owed as $20. I had never been so happy to see a medical bill. I couldn't believe that an emergency room would give me a price *before* the treatment. And I couldn't believe the price was so reasonable. I mean, they had us right where they wanted us. Defenseless. Weren't they going to exploit our desperation and rip us off?

My head was spinning from the kindness as we entered the exam room. But we weren't out of the woods yet. Here came the doctor. I gave him a suspicious look, but to my shock he didn't press us to get a CT scan. Yup—looks like a migraine that calls for some stronger pain meds, he said. We could buy the drugs at the hospital pharmacy when we headed for home, he added.

This is where they're going to get us, I thought to myself. I know how hospitals jack up the price of medication. But they got me again. About twenty minutes later we happily forked over about $30 cash for two prescriptions. Totally reasonable.

We walked out the door with the extraordinary feeling of a hospital caring for both our physical and our financial well-being. If only every other American could experience this feeling. Unfortunately, they'd have to travel across the world. You see, we weren't at a hospital in the United States. We were more than seven thousand miles from home. We were on vacation in Africa, getting treated at the Nairobi Hospital in Kenya.

You may know the pain of overpriced health care in the United States. And even if you aren't aware of it, price gouging is so common in American medicine that you've certainly been a victim of it. You usually can't see the prices before you undergo treatment, and by the time you do it's too late. You feel socked in the gut and they're telling you to pay up. In this chapter I'll show you how to save big money by finding the best prices for the care you need. You can often pay less without compromising quality.

Kenya taught me something important about health care in the United States. Kenya is one of the poorest countries in the world. It's so underdeveloped that its roads are pocked with holes, the tap water is unsafe to drink, and electricity gets rationed. And yet, somehow, the Nairobi Hospital has figured out how to give a patient a fair price *before* the treatment is provided.

The Nairobi Hospital made me feel wistful about American health care. And it also ticked me off. Obviously, American hospitals and clinics and other medical facilities *could* figure out how to provide a fair price up front to patients. But the industry has opposed such commonsense openness about prices.

Imagine if other industries behaved with this type of secrecy. Instead of negotiating with the car dealer you'd sign a document that says you agree to cover all charges associated with the vehicle and drive it off the lot. You could pick an economy car like a Honda and get hit months later with the bill for a Lamborghini. And you'd be on the hook for it.

If I am going to *pay* for a Lambo at least I want to *get* a Lambo. But that's not how the American health care industry works. Various forms of price gouging have become standard. It's enabled by the hidden prices and a business model that's based on tricking you into paying more than you should.

Somehow it's been accepted to use these tactics to profit from the pain and sickness of you and your loved ones. The deviance has been normalized. The industry fights any efforts that would make prices open, so you need to protect yourself and know how to find a fair price. It takes extra effort, but sadly it falls on us. It's not fair and no way for a civilized country to operate, but this is the system the power players in the medical industry have created and continue to protect. Remember what I said in chapter one, where I provide five reasons we need to fight this system: Our health care system isn't broken. It was made this way. The business side of the industry is intent on taking advantage of you. But you can take steps to protect yourself and save big money in the process.

Put a limit on what you agree to pay for emergency care.

Imagine waking up in the dark early hours of the morning to the smell of smoke. You run to the top of your stairs and see your living room catching fire down below. Your couch, curtains—everything is getting ignited. Your family scurries down the stairs and out the front door unharmed. You escaped!

To your relief, the fire department arrives within minutes. Your precious possessions can be saved. But then the firefighters stand by the side of the truck while the battalion chief approaches you with a clipboard. It's the fire department's financial services agreement. "I agree to be financially responsible for payment for the department's services," it says.

"Sign here," the battalion chief says, handing you a pen.

You're incredulous. "This is no time for paperwork!" you shout, pointing to the flames that you can see through your living-room window. "How much is this going to cost?" you scream at the battalion chief.

"No way to tell until after the fire," the battalion chief replies, shrugging his shoulders. He points to the side of his truck and you realize it's a *for-profit* fire department. The tagline on the truck says NO PAY, NO SPRAY.[1]

You don't have time to debate what it should cost—the flames are licking your kitchen cupboards. And your possessions are priceless.

You can't hesitate for another second. You sign the paperwork. Whatever—just put out the fire! You're so desperate you'd pay anything.

Depending on a for-profit fire department is obviously a problem if your house is ablaze. Most fire departments don't operate that way for good reason. Homeowners would be so desperate they'd be easy to exploit. But that's just how it is when we undergo a medical emergency.

Dr. Eric Bricker likes to use the for-profit fire department analogy to illustrate how the medical industry treats patients. Our society protects us in other cases when we are in desperate need of a product or service. But when it comes to health care, we are left vulnerable to price gouging and exploitation. Bricker, who lives near Dallas, is an internal medicine doctor who also has a health care finance background. He cofounded and then sold Compass Professional Health Services (now called Alight Solutions), a company that helped employers and workers find quality health care at the best value.[2]

With most products and services, Bricker explained, the law of supply and demand can keep prices in check. If there's enough of something available on the market, consumers will buy from the place with the best price. That rewards the sellers, who reduce their prices, and penalizes anyone who tries to gouge the customer.

But the demand for health care is much different, Bricker said. In some cases, a patient is like a homeowner watching her house go up in flames. Let's say she's suffering from cancer. She must pay for treatment no matter the price, or else she'll die. Same with a man suffering a heart attack. He can't wait for treatment. He will pay anything to save his life.

Economists call this type of need inelastic demand, Bricker said, because it doesn't change if prices go up or down. That's why the medical industry can get away with charging us so much and continue raising the prices. You and I will pay anything to save our lives or the lives of those we love.[3]

The health care industry exploits inelastic demand to maximize its profit. Millions of diabetics embody inelastic demand because they can't simply say "no thank you" to the insulin they need to survive. But we've seen the price of insulin more than triple between 2007 and 2017.[4] Those patients and their families have had to keep digging deeper into their wallets, or going into debt, to find a way to pay the price, any price, to stay alive. Often, they can't. People with type 1 diabetes are at an increased risk of sickness and premature death because they can't afford the price of insulin, experts have found.[5] This is just one example.[6] Selfishness and greed have become rampant in the industry, Bricker said. "It's a situation where people and corporations can exploit pain and suffering for profit," he said.

This brings me back to the moral problem that's at the root of so many of these issues. It's immoral to take advantage of someone who is so desperate for health care that they will pay any price. And yet this immorality is a foundation of the American medical industry. You've probably heard of the Golden Rule: "Do unto others as you would have them do unto you." It's based on the words of Jesus, recorded in the Bible, in Matthew 7:12. This principle resonates deeply to me as a Christian. But it's not just a Christian belief. People from all different faith backgrounds and worldviews believe that we shouldn't be selfish and exploit others. It's a foundation of human decency that often seems like it's been lost on the business side of the American health care industry.

So what can we do? We are not helpless. It just means we are forced to play defense instead of offense, especially when we need emergency treatment. We are particularly vulnerable to getting price gouged in an emergency room because we don't have time to quibble about the details. But there's a method you and your loved ones can use as a first line of defense.

At some point early in that visit to the emergency room you're going to get presented with a document you need to sign, giving consent to treatment and agreeing to pay the cost for the care. The problem is that you don't know how much care you'll need, and no one tells you the prices. If you're uninsured that means you're on the hook for whatever they charge. If you're insured, then you could be hit with a bill for whatever your insurance company does not cover. And if some of the doctors who treat you do not have contracts with the hospital, you could be required to pay a portion of exorbitant out-of-network bills. Even crazier—sometimes the in-network rates negotiated by your insurer are outrageously high.

Quizzify, a health literacy company, convened several experts to discuss what patients can do to protect themselves from outrageous medical bills for any nonelective care, such as a trip to the emergency room.[7] Al Lewis, cofounder and CEO of Quizzify, says patients need to add what he calls "the mother of all informed consent" language to the document the patients or their loved ones sign at the time they give permission to give treatment. Patients need to write this clause on the informed consent document: **"I consent to appropriate treatment and (including applicable**

insurance payments) to be responsible for reasonable charges up to two times the Medicare rate." Take a photo of it for your records.

If the hospital pushes back, Lewis pointed out that federal law requires hospitals to provide emergency treatment to patients who need it, whether or not they sign a financial consent form. And if a bill came in at an outrageous amount and was disputed, the patient would be able to show to an arbitrator or in court that a reasonable offer was made for payment.

Medicare, the government's insurance plan for people who are disabled or over age sixty-five, sets prices for the services it funds. Those prices are typically much lower than what an uninsured person is charged, or what a commercial insurance company negotiates. Medicare prices create a nice benchmark for a fair price we should be willing to pay. Even if we pay twice the Medicare rate it's a good deal compared with how much they could charge if we don't set a limit.

Adding this clause to your legal agreement to treatment is no guarantee. But it puts a ceiling on the amount that you say you are willing to pay. Lewis said he knows of cases where it's been successful. You hope it will protect you from outrageous bills. And if you still get hit with outrageous bills, it will give you legal grounds to contest them, to the hospital and in court, if necessary, as I discussed in part one of this book.

Use Medicare prices as a guide.

The price variation gets even more insidious by making working Americans pay the highest prices. The amount you pay largely depends on your insurance coverage, or perhaps your lack of coverage. The government health plans, Medicare and Medicaid, tend to have lower prices. The commercial health plans that cover working Americans tend to have higher prices, often many times more than the government plans.[8]

We discourage other forms of discrimination in the United States, but it's become the standard way of operating in the health care industry. It would be like McDonald's saying Big Macs are $4 for anyone over age sixty-five but from $8 to $40 for anyone younger.

There's no reason you should have to pay more than Medicare would pay for the same services just because of your age. Discrimination is wrong, so you and I should fight it—even in health care pricing. You can do this by finding out what Medicare pays for a particular service. That's easy if a hospital has posted its prices. But otherwise it may be tedious. But it is public information, so you have a right to know it.

When you have the Medicare price in hand it gives you a leg up when you're looking for your own fair price. It also gives you leverage to ask for a better deal. The information is particularly handy if you're uninsured or covered by a high-deductible health plan that requires you to pay a lot of money before the coverage kicks in.

The medical facilities don't initially charge patients different amounts. They use what they call their chargemaster to come up with their sticker price. They levy this amount on everyone—and it's typically many times more than they would be willing to receive for a given service. What's actually paid is determined by a discount on the chargemaster rate that's negotiated by each insurance carrier. The negotiated rates can vary widely determined by how much leverage the hospital or carrier has in the negotiations. That's why some insurance companies will pay much more than others for the same service at the same hospital.

Medicare, on the other hand, sets its prices for doctors and hospitals. It can do this because it's the largest single payer in the market, so the medical community needs its revenue to survive. There's some debate in the industry about whether Medicare rates are fair. Doctors and hospitals love to complain about them. But they are carefully set by experts who determine their fairness, and they're adjusted for regional differences, such as labor costs. They also factor in the sickness of individual patients. And here's another fact: The hospitals and other medical providers accept the Medicare rates. Maybe even more important, they are publicly available, so we can see the Medicare prices. That makes them a good comparison for us when we get medical care.

The reformers fighting for fair prices often use Medicare rates to highlight the industry's discrimination against working Americans on commercial insurance plans. A recent RAND Corporation study, funded by Employers' Forum of Indiana, a coalition that's working to improve the value payers and patients receive from the industry, found wide variation in what employers and patients are paying for the same services.[9] Employers were paying from less than two times the Medicare rate on the low end to more than three and a half times the Medicare rate on the high end for hospital care, the study found. In other words, if Medicare paid $100 the employers would pay between $200 and $350 for the same thing. The large hospitals' systems tended to have the highest prices, the study said. Overall, employers paid about 358 percent more than the Medicare rate for outpatient care, meaning the types of services that didn't require an overnight stay. Prices were more than six times higher than the Medicare rates at one facility.

RAND researchers produced a follow-up that found that in 2018, employers and private insurers paid 247 percent of what Medicare would have paid for the same services, across all hospital and outpatient services.[10] That was an increase from what they paid in the previous two years and was due to consolidation in the health care markets, which gives providers leverage to charge higher prices, the report said. The price hikes were not related to better quality, the researchers found.

If the private payers included in the study had been allowed to pay Medicare rates, their spending would have been reduced by 58 percent. Between 2016 and 2018, that would have saved them $19.7 billion.

So how do you get the Medicare price? It's easy if a hospital is complying with the federal government's requirement to post the information on its website. But if not, you can try going to the Medicare website and downloading the Procedure Price Lookup Comparison File.[11] That's an Excel spreadsheet that provides the national average total payment Medicare makes for almost four thousand services and procedures in ambulatory surgical centers and hospital outpatient departments. The prices will be an estimate of what Medicare would pay in your area because the actual payments get adjusted based on the part of the country.

You can also try the Medicare outpatient procedure cost lookup tool.[12] Type in the name of the procedure or the billing code to see the total cost paid by Medicare. I looked up a colonoscopy and saw that Medicare's total cost is listed at $715 in an ambulatory surgical center and $1,212 in a hospital outpatient department. Again, it provides national averages, so the cost may be higher or lower in your part of the country.

The Medicare rates may only give you an approximation of what the federal government health plan would pay for a particular service at your nearby facility. To be specific, you could also ask your hospital or outpatient facility to tell you what they get paid by Medicare for the procedure, and then tell them you'd like the same price.

Find the lowest prices for scans, tests, and treatment—it's usually not at a hospital. Also, check the cash price.

Prices may vary greatly for the same images or tests or procedures performed in different types of facilities. Procedures performed in ambulatory surgical centers cost Medicare about half of what they cost in hospitals, according to the American Academy of Orthopedic Surgeons.[13] The median price for an MRI in a hospital compared with a freestanding imaging center could vary by thousands of dollars.[14] This kind of hidden price variation is the baseline way the industry operates. It's everywhere.

Typically, hospitals will add fees that make you pay more for the same services you could get at an outpatient surgery or imaging center. There is no proof that the big brand-name hospitals are providing superior care, unless it's for a medical emergency or some type of complex care. And even when researchers compare high-price hospitals with lower-price hospitals they do not find that the higher prices are associated with better-quality care. You're just paying more for the same thing.[15, 16]

In other words—paying more for many drugs or medical procedures is not like paying more for a luxury automobile or a bigger and better house.

Thus, the first question you can ask when you need a non-emergency test or procedure or medication is this: **Where can I get this for the best price?**

Assuming it isn't an emergency, you can get an estimate of the fair price for a test or procedure and then try to find out what your doctor or hospital will make you pay with your insurance plan, or in cash if you're uninsured or on a high-deductible plan. Elsewhere in this book I have mentioned that the websites FairHealthConsumer.org and HealthcareBluebook.com are good resources to get price estimates for a test or procedure in your part of the country. Your doctor should be able to give you a clear description of what they are ordering, and their billing department should be able to easily give you the billing code so you can be sure to make the right price comparison. If it's a service by the doctor or an outpatient facility, like a walk-in clinic or surgery center, it will be a CPT code that describes what you need. If it's a hospital procedure that requires an overnight stay they might use an ICD-10-PCS code.

FairHealthConsumer.org gives you an estimated price that's based on the negotiated and out-of-network rates of insurers in that area. If you're uninsured, then you should expect the starting price to be at the out-of-network estimate. But it's important to remember that all prices are negotiable. Sometimes cash-paying patients can get a deal that's better than what insured patients would pay. It saves doctors and hospitals a lot of time and hassle if they don't have to wait for an insurance company to send a check or wrangle them over a payment. Every patient should ask for the cash price, even if they have insurance.

HealthcareBluebook.com price estimates are based on what others have paid for those services, so it's a good benchmark for what would be fair for you to pay.

Whenever you're looking at these sites that provide price estimates, they might not have the precise procedure you are looking for or be available in your location. But they should give you an estimate of what a fair price should be.

As I have mentioned, we should also now be able to get many price estimates from hospital websites. In June 2019 President Donald Trump issued an executive order that required increased price and quality transparency in health care, so patients could make informed decisions about where they go for care.[17] Hospitals and insurance plans are required under the rules associated with the order to provide prices and cost sharing information to patients.

The new rules have already been a big breakthrough, even though compliance by hospitals has been spotty so far. Hospitals were required to start posting prices for common procedures in 2021. But the financial penalty for hospitals that don't comply is small. Some hospitals might consider it more profitable to avoid posting the prices.

Many hospitals have complied with the Trump order by posting rates for patients who pay cash or are covered by various commercial health insurance carriers or Medicare. Check all the hospitals nearby because they may have much cheaper or more expensive prices for the same types of treatment. The new federal requirement gives each of us the ability to demand the prices, even if they haven't posted them.

Whenever possible, save money by getting a test or treatment or scan at an ambulatory surgical center or freestanding testing center or laboratory. Avoid any facility that's connected to a hospital, if you can. Those hospital fees are something we can often avoid.

Whenever possible, stay in network with your insurance plan.

If you have health insurance, make sure, if possible, that you avoid getting care with hospitals and other medical providers that do not have contracted rates with your insurance plan. These out-of-network medical providers can pretty much charge whatever they want to your insurance plan. Then you may have to pay a larger share than you would have, had you stayed in-network. It's been the practice of some medical providers to come after patients for the balance. These are the notorious "balance" or "surprise" bills that can easily sneak up on patients, and they're often for outrageous amounts.

Congress passed a ban on surprise medical bills at the end of 2020 that will require the bills to go to mediation to determine what should be paid. Hopefully, the ban will help, though some say it will still result in high costs. But out-of-network bills will likely still be with us, so try to stay in network.

Sometimes it's impossible to avoid out-of-network care, like if you go to an in-network hospital for emergency care and get treated by an out-of-network doctor. You can't possibly prevent that. But other times we can prevent it, like if we're looking for a doctor or a facility where we can get treatment for ourselves or our loved ones. In those cases, we must do everything we can to stay in network so we can take advantage of the rates that have been set by our insurance plan. Make sure you always ask for the cash price, if possible, because sometimes it's even lower than the negotiated insurance rates, as I discuss in the following chapter. But start by staying in network.

Check with both the health care provider and your insurance company to make sure the treatment will be in network. Their agreements can change at any time, or the person on the phone at your doctor's office or hospital might not be properly informed. If you have health coverage, make sure you call your insurance company or the company administering your organization's self-funded health plan. (Most American workers and their families are covered by self-funded plans, which means you should consult your organization's benefits department and executives if you're running into problems.) Once you have the medical code that's used to describe the test or treatment you will receive, ask whether your insurance plan covers the service at a given location, and what your price will be after treatment. You want to make sure that whatever is being recommended is covered, and you also want to be able to see if you might be able to pay less *without* using your insurance, as I will describe in the following chapter.

Try GoodRx and Good Shepherd Pharmacy for your medication.

If you want to see how crazy health care price variation can get, try calling different pharmacies and asking for their prices for the same drug. Pharmacist Phil Baker and his team at Good Shepherd Pharmacy in Memphis, Tennessee, did just that, and the results were eye-opening. They picked eleven common generic drugs and looked up what it would cost for a ninety-day supply on the website GoodRx.com, which provides coupons for discounts on drugs that can be filled at different pharmacies. Then they compared the GoodRx coupon prices to the cash prices for the same medications at Walgreens, Kroger, Walmart, Publix, and Costco.

The price variation was astonishing. Walgreens sold the acid reflux drug Pantoprazole 40 mg for $305.89 for a ninety-day supply. Kroger had the lowest cash price for the same drug among the pharmacies at $90.99. And the GoodRx price was $13.77.

Walgreens wanted $737.89 for a ninety-day supply of the cholesterol drug Atorvastatin 40 mg. Costco had it for $29.53 and GoodRx for $15.27.

If you just paid cash at one of the pharmacies for a ninety-day supply for all the drugs in the analysis, Costco came out as the cheapest at $194.87.

Drug prices—for the same medication—will vary at different pharmacies. The GoodRx price is a coupon you would take to a specific pharmacy. And often, Baker's team found, the GoodRx coupon would be for a dramatically lower price than the cash price of the very pharmacy where the coupon would be filled. For example, the stomach acid drug Pantoprazole 40 mg was offered for $90.99 at Kroger. But, as I mentioned above, Kroger would sell the same thing with a GoodRx coupon for thirteen bucks and change.

The GoodRx price was the lowest for almost every drug, which shows why it's always good to check it. "GoodRx is a great option if you need one drug, one time," Baker said.

But Baker doesn't recommend using GoodRx for all your drugs because that would require filling your prescriptions at multiple pharmacies. You want your pharmacist to be able to see all the drugs you're taking in case some of them interact in a way that's not safe. Also, keep in mind if you use a GoodRx coupon what you spend will not contribute to your insurance plan's annual deductible because you won't be running the payment through your insurance.

If you're uninsured or on a low income or on a sharing or a high-deductible health plan, you may also want to check out Good Shepherd's membership plan. Members pay $5 per month for a ninety-day supply of any of the 350 generic drugs the pharmacy keeps in stock. For uninsured patients, Good Shepherd can get special pricing on brand-name and specialty drugs by working with international pharmacies and manufacturer assistance programs. Brand-name drugs and insulin are priced at $25 a month for patients who qualify. Baker said if the fees are too high, uninsured patients can qualify for additional financial assistance.

Every person's medication needs are different, so the main thing to remember is that you should check GoodRx to compare prices at the different pharmacies in your area. And also, if you're uninsured or on a high-deductible or health sharing plan, see if you're eligible for the Good Shepherd program. It may be a good solution for you.

Don't assume your insurer is protecting you.

Do not expect your insurance company to fight on your behalf to get you the best price. It may benefit when you pay more. Michael Frank discovered all this the hard way. His physical recovery from a 2015 partial hip replacement suffered a psychological setback when he got the bill. His insurer, Aetna, had agreed to pay NYU Langone Medical Center in New York City more than $70,000 for the procedure. He had a high-deductible plan, so he got billed for more than $7,000 of the total.

Michael has a square jaw, neatly trimmed salt-and-pepper hair, and the no-nonsense intensity you'd expect from a New Yorker who is getting ripped off. He also isn't the kind of guy you want to argue with about finances. He isn't afraid to read the fine print and has the expertise to interpret it. He's worked for the insurance industry for more than three decades and is the former president of the Actuarial Society of Greater New York. He's taught actuarial science at Columbia University and leads seminars for insurance regulators. Most of us would shut up and beg for a payment plan. Michael dug in for the fight.

Aetna promised Michael that he had been given the special in-network member rate the insurer had negotiated with the hospital. These discounted rates are the way insurers say they reward the faithful people who pay them premiums each month. But what insurers don't advertise is that they pay hospitals wildly different rates for the same procedures. Michael was able to see that Medicare, the federal government insurance plan, which makes its prices public, would have paid the hospital about $20,000 for the same procedure. The nonprofit FAIR Health, which also publishes pricing benchmarks, estimated the total fee should have been about $29,000—and that price included all the surgeon fees.

I sat in Michael's home office and he showed me the reams of paperwork, organized in thick binders and tabbed with yellow sticky notes to mark key details. The hospital's sticker price, including the surgeon and anesthesiologist, had been $138,000, but that's just the chargemaster rate—a price that hospitals set as high as they want so it looks like they are giving insurance companies a discount. Michael scanned the billing codes and showed me various red flags: charges for physical therapy sessions that never happened and drugs he never received. The cost of the implant and related supplies was listed at $26,068. Michael called and emailed the device company until he reached a rep who told him the device cost should be around $1,500, and his surgeon confirmed the amount to him. He had five sutures, and each had been reimbursed by the insurer at $2,600, for a total of $13,000.

"I believe that I am a victim of excessive billing," Michael wrote to Aetna. He assumed Aetna would share his concern. Aetna reviewed the case twice but stood by its payment of the bills. The payment was appropriate, the company told him. He got nowhere with his complaints.

The overpriced operation—and the insurer's willingness to pay it—illustrates the role the carriers play in our rising health care costs. They often agree to high prices and then pass the costs on to patients in the form of higher premiums and out-of-pocket costs. And they rake in massive profits. The year after Michael's operation his rates went up almost 19 percent.

The insurers make more money when health care prices increase. The Affordable Care Act, the 2010 law often referred to as Obamacare, included a provision that tried to keep insurance companies' profit margins in check. The "medical loss ratio" said insurers had to spend at least 80 percent of what they took in from premiums on medical care. That sounds like a good idea, because it limits ridiculous administrative costs and profit margins. But it also contributes to rising health care costs. Insurance companies like to say their profit margins are small, and that may be the case. But their duty and obligation are to make the company money, not save yours. So let's say they just give themselves a 3 percent profit. In that case, the company increases its revenue by spending more.

It's as if a mom told her son he could have only 3 percent of a bowl of ice cream. A clever child would say, "Make it a bigger bowl."

That means the more we pay, the more insurance companies profit. Policy wonks call this a perverse incentive. The hospitals and the insurance carriers make more money as health care costs go higher, whether or not the costs are justified. And the problem, as Michael found, is that patients and employers are typically not allowed to see the price of treatment before they undergo it. The payment involves four parties—the patient, the employer, the hospital, and the insurance carrier. But only two parties—the hospital and the carrier—have agreed to a price. That means the patient and the employer pay a price that they had no role in negotiating. In a sense, the industry stakeholders are collaborating against the people funding the system, which is one reason prices keep climbing unchecked. "The system," Michael told me, "is stacked against the consumer."

His disillusionment with his insurance company illustrates a common feeling among Americans. The consumer intelligence company J.D. Power found that 60 percent of privately insured Americans were not contacted by their insurer with information about COVID-19. Almost half said their health plan did not show concern for their health during the pandemic. Health plans are "widely perceived" as "not putting the best interests of their members first," said one of the people who conducted the survey.[18]

Demand that your health care providers post their prices.

I like how Dr. Mark Friedman describes what he considers the ultimate solution for the cost shifting and price gouging of working Americans that's become standard in the medical industry. "Everyone talks about a single-payer system," Friedman told me. "We need a single-price system."

Friedman has had a varied career. He's an emergency room doctor and has been a hospital's chief of emergency medicine, a chief executive of a claims analytics company, and a medical school professor. He's now the chief medical officer at First Stop Health, a telemedicine company in Chicago. He's spent decades in the industry and said nothing would be better than requiring doctors' offices and hospitals to simply have a single price for their services that's posted, so everyone can see it. When he takes his car to the shop, he can see how much it costs to get the brakes done, he said. If he doesn't like the price, he can take it elsewhere. And when they've done the job, he knows what he needs to pay. No tricks. No surprises. Currently, the commercial insurance companies can vary their rates because they hide them, so people can't tell when they're paying more for the same thing. Requiring a single price would eliminate much of the administrative hassle and high cost that comes with medical billing. There would be no discounts, no negotiating, no repricing of claims, no confusion about codes. Monopolies would be destroyed, he said, because facilities and companies would lose their leverage.

Until the prices become public in a consistent, clear, and understandable way, patients need to come up with some health care hacks to work around the problem. It's important that we push for the prices so the industry knows we expect them and so we can make informed decisions.

It can feel overwhelming to try to obtain the information you need to get the best value for what you spend on medical care. The industry has made it difficult for us on purpose—so it can continue to exploit our ignorance. We need to demand that the prices for health care services be made available wherever possible. Call the board members of your local hospital—they're the ones responsible for how the facility is run—and ask why they don't post their prices. Do the same with freestanding imaging and surgery centers.

Health policy experts often talk about how patients don't do their homework or won't take the time to do the type of research required to understand the system. I think that's a condescending and paternalistic perspective. When patients understand what's at stake and how the system is working against them, they're highly motivated to push ahead to get the care they need for themselves and their loved ones. And while it is difficult for individuals to beat the system, our employers have much greater leverage and some are already leading the fight against price gouging—and they're winning.

We need to reward the medical providers who offer fair prices with our business. We need to ditch the medical providers who are price gouging. When we do, we cut off the oxygen they need to survive. They will have to lower their prices and share them with us if they want us to give them our business. Maybe then the American health care system will start to live up to the fair pricing standards that have been set at the Nairobi Hospital.

TAKE ACTION

1. Write in this clause when you sign your financial agreements when you are getting emergency treatment at a hospital: "I consent to appropriate treatment and (including applicable insurance payments) to be responsible for reasonable charges up to two times the Medicare rate."
2. If you have insurance, make sure that you go to an in-network medical provider whenever you can. That will protect you from high out-of-network bills.
3. Get the billing codes in advance that will be used for whatever procedure or treatment you need. Your doctor or hospital should be able to provide the codes. Ask what

the cash price would be for the service. Ask how much it will cost with your insurance, if you are covered. Go to FairHealthConsumer.org and HealthcareBluebook.com to see what the sites say health plans are paying for the services. If you're insured, make sure your plan covers what you are receiving.

4. See if hospitals near you have complied with the federal government's requirement to post their prices. Check multiple facilities because they might charge less or more for the same thing. If hospitals or other medical facilities aren't posting their prices, demand that they do. If you can, avoid high-price hospitals.

5. Hint: You can usually get *much* better prices by *avoiding* hospitals or facilities associated with hospitals. They often add excessive fees.

6. Try GoodRx and Good Shepherd Pharmacy for your medications.

7. Ask your provider if they will give you a break on the price if you pay up front in cash. Medical providers are fed up with insurance carriers, so they may give a discount if you don't use your insurance. I discuss this in the following chapter.

8

You Might Save Money by *Not* Using Your Insurance

Y OUR HEALTH INSURERS PROMISE TO save you big money by using their influence in the marketplace to get you the best possible prices on medical care. But that may not be the case. In recent years people have found they sometimes get a better deal if they don't use their insurance plan. This chapter will show how it plays out in a variety of circumstances: medical imaging, supplies, drugs, and more. It may work for you in different ways than it does for other people. And going without your insurance coverage may save you money in some cases and show no benefit in others. But here's the bottom line: **Always ask for the cash price.**

Your insurance plan's discount may be unimpressive.

I love Dr. Zubin Damania, the influencer and entertainer who goes by the nickname ZDoggMD. His irreverent and unflinching take on health care, through music videos and commentary and interviews, is entertaining, informative, and outrage inducing. Damania is a Stanford-trained internist and health care reformer, but even he can't always protect himself and his family from the hidden price hikes that sometimes come with an insurance plan.

Damania had his family on a high-deductible plan in the fall of 2020. That meant he had to pay $6,000 out of pocket before his health benefits would start to pay for anything. His nine-year-old daughter needed an MRI, so he called the large local health care system nearby and asked how much it would cost. He and the customer service representative sorted out which billing code would be used for the test. The rep said the cost would be $1,600.

Damania asked if he would get a discount for paying cash instead of running it through his insurance. It's a savvy question we should all ask every time we go to the doctor because it might be a good way to save money. The cash pay discount would be 30 percent, the rep told him.

Damania weighed his options. He could pay cash and save $480. That's a good savings. But then his insurance company would not apply whatever he paid to his deductible, the amount he had to pay each year before the coverage would kick in. So that may cause him to pay more down the road. His other option was to run the MRI through his insurance plan to take advantage of the discount his insurance company had made with the medical provider. Insurance companies get us to pay monthly premiums on the promise that they are getting us great discounts off the exorbitant sticker prices offered by doctors and hospitals. The problem is that insurance companies negotiate their discounts with medical providers in secret. That meant Damania would have no way of knowing the discount in advance. He mulled it over and decided his insurance company's negotiated discount had to be better than the 30 percent cash discount. Also, running it through his insurance would also apply to his deductible. Using his insurance plan should be the best on both fronts.

Damania billed the MRI through his insurance plan. Then came the shocker. His insurance company's negotiated discount turned out to be zero. Nothing. No discount. His insurance plan required him to pay the full $1,600.

Damania mocks the absurdities of American health care for a living, but even he was scratching his head. "What's the point of paying tens of thousands for family health insurance if the insurer, with all their leverage, can't negotiate a better price than I can," Damania said to me. "I guess that's why we have the most expensive health care in the world."

Insurers have led us to believe they get us the best deals. That's one way they promote their products to individuals and employers who sign us up for their plans. But the prices they negotiate are subject to so much behind-the-scenes horse trading and so many side deals that what's best for their members might get overlooked. Patients, of course, have no idea how the haggling between health care titans affects what they pay. Keeping everything behind closed doors allows all the players in the medical industry to dodge any specific questions about their profits, or why they're all making us pay so much in the first place. This madness helps explain why you may pay more running medical care through your insurance carrier than you would paying out of pocket.

Not everyone with insurance is going to be interested in paying cash. It is the most obvious thing to try if you have a high deductible—and that's an increasingly large number of people. The federal government estimates that almost half of Americans with employment-based insurance coverage are in these types of plans.[1] Experts consider a deductible high if it's more than $1,300 for an individual and $2,600 for a family. But paying cash may also be a consideration for medical supplies, or if your health benefits require a copayment for drugs. Believe it or not, the cash price for drugs may even be less than a $10 copay you fork over at the counter at the pharmacy.[2] Getting the cash price is also essential if you are uninsured or covered by a health sharing plan that requires you to pay a portion of the costs up front.

When Harry Sit was living in San Jose, California, in 2019, he discovered the absurdity of health insurance–negotiated rates after his wife noticed a worrisome spot on his scalp. He'd had similar spots before and had had to get them checked to make sure they weren't cancerous. But he had recently changed his health plan. He had a $6,000 deductible. That meant he would be paying out of pocket for the examination whether or not he ran it through his insurance. He also realized his dermatologist was no longer in network, meaning the doctor didn't have an agreed-upon rate with his insurance company. That meant he might have to pay a much higher price.

He had something to compare it with. A few years before the same dermatologist had checked out the same type of spot on Sit's skin. He got the in-network discount but still had to pay the whole cost because of his high deductible. At that time, his insurer's discount got him a price of $360.

This time he did not run the same procedure with the same dermatologist through his insurance plan. He braced himself for what he assumed would be a larger bill. But somehow the price was less: $161.

Same doctor. Same examination. But less than half the cost without insurance than he had previously paid with insurance.

As Damania pointed out, it's important to note that if you pay cash the money you spend won't be applied against your deductible. In Sit's case that was not as important because his deductible was so high he didn't expect to meet it, unless his family had serious unexpected health problems. But someone with a lower deductible might want any money they spend to help pay down the deductible, so they can start having the insurance plan shoulder the costs. People with lower deductibles might want to think more about paying cash toward the end of the year, when it's clear their deductible won't be met.

Sit, who now runs his own search firm to help people find financial advisers, said it's no surprise that things would cost more with health insurance than they would without. The same thing is true when you need to get your car windshield repaired, he pointed out. The shop will ask if you're paying cash or running it through insurance. And if you're using insurance the price will be much higher because medical providers will try to take all they can get. "Insurance companies are seen as having deep pockets," Sit said. "It would be foolish for them not to grab the money."

Your insurers' rates are set by wacky hidden side deals. See if you can get a better deal paying cash.

Prices may be especially high at the marquee medical facilities that dominate many cities. They leverage their brand name and size when they're negotiating their reimbursement prices with insurers. These hospital systems know employers want their services included in their plans, even if there are other suitable medical providers in town. So they demand higher rates. Research shows it's even worse if the health systems have consolidated, because it gives them more leverage to jack up prices.[3]

The big-name medical systems "tend to be very aggressive in their negotiations," one seasoned negotiator for insurance companies told me.[4] Sometimes the concessions get so out of hand the insurers agree to pay higher prices for some services in exchange for lower prices for others. The smaller or more independent medical providers then try to draw in patients and insurers by accepting lower prices.

Here's how crazy it can get: Sometimes insurance companies agree to pay *more* than what got billed for a medical service. When the State of Tennessee had a vendor, ClaimInformatics, analyze the payments by its health care plan, which were administered by BlueCross BlueShield of Tennessee, it found about ninety-six thousand cases where the plan paid more than what was billed. The claims were worth $1.8 million. The BlueCross BlueShield chief operating officer responded with a letter in which he admitted they sometimes pay more than what's billed. BlueCross saves money for the plan by paying certain providers a contracted flat rate, whether it's above or below what the provider billed, the COO wrote.[5]

I reached out to the BlueCross plan and they told me that the COO was talking only about chiropractic bills, where they paid a flat rate that was sometimes higher than the billed charge, and that the arrangement had saved millions of dollars. But I ran that by ClaimInformatics and they said it wasn't just chiropractic bills where they saw that BlueCross had overpaid.

The crazy insurance industry billing games take other unexpected forms that will cost you big bucks. There's a lot of behind-the-scenes haggling between insurance companies and hospitals, for example, where insurers might agree to pay more than they should for certain services so they can get a better deal on others.

In the old days we didn't have to worry about the prices with or without insurance. But the health care marketplace is always evolving and shifting. In 1960 only half of all hospital care in the United States was covered by an insurance plan, and almost all prescription drugs were paid for out of pocket.[6] Over the decades insurance plans increasingly took over, but our monthly premiums were taking care of the cost of our care. But the prices keep on rising, beyond what our monthly premiums can cover. And rather than push back and demand lower prices, our employers have merely passed the cost on to workers in the form of high deductibles and copays and reduced coverage. They keep monthly premiums somewhat in check and just make us pay more. This means that many insured Americans are functionally uninsured. Anyone who is paying the up-front cost should demand to know the price of every drug, test, or treatment.

Dr. Johnny Luo told me he often sees patients getting better deals without using their insurance. He runs a business called Doctor's Choice in Warwick, Rhode Island, which helps older adults navigate the health care system. He's often looking for the best options to help patients save money. The scenarios always vary by what a patient needs and their type of insurance, but he's seeing price inflation with insurance across the board. For example, in one case he looked up a drug called Benzonatate that's used for a chronic cough, and he found it would cost the patient $137.72 out of pocket with insurance. But Walmart sold the same drug for $10 cash. Somehow the drug was thirteen times more with insurance than it was without. "That just baffles me," he said. "It's crazy, but in this situation it's actually more expensive to have insurance than it is to not have insurance."

Luo said he often sees cheaper cash prices with certain medication for headaches, acid reflux, and skin conditions. He suspects they get priced higher by insurers because the carriers want to ward off the possibly sick patients who need them. Or it may happen when insurers lock in their prices over the long term, he said, only to have the drug price drop.

Luo said cash prices may also be better for other medical services. A doctor's office or imaging center or blood lab saves a lot of money collecting their payments when patients pay cash, Luo said. Most medical providers aren't big enough to do their own collections, and they pay a hefty rate just to farm out that work to someone else. When a patient pays cash up front, the medical providers can make more without the hassle.

Check your hospital's cash pay prices.

I've mentioned elsewhere in this book that the federal government has given us a powerful tool to check hospital prices. Starting January 1, 2021, hospitals were required to post to their websites their cash prices and negotiated prices with insurance companies. I recently saw the dramatic power of this information. A young woman had contacted me after receiving an exorbitant medical bill for a trip to her local hospital's emergency room. She had sliced her finger while cutting an avocado and received three stitches during the brief ER visit. She was covered by her company's self-funded insurance plan, which was administered by one of the big insurance companies, and it was an in-network visit. Looking at her insurance documents, she could see the insurer's negotiated rate came to $3,101 paid by her health plan. She got a bill for an additional $2,670. So the hospital would be paid $5,771 for three stitches based on the insurer's negotiated rate. That's almost $2,000 per stitch!

I showed her how to obtain the billing codes they used on her claim. Then we checked the hospital's website and saw the facility had complied with the new requirement to post its prices. We looked up the billing code that made up the biggest chunk of the charges, the CPT code 99283, for a level 3 emergency room visit. The hospital listed her insurer's negotiated rate as $5,805 for that code, which explains why her bill was so massive. But the cash price for the same level 3 code was $256.84. In other words, her insurer's negotiated rate was twenty-two times higher than what the patient would have paid in cash.

Check your insurer's markups on your medical supplies.

You may also save money bypassing your insurance plan to pay for medical supplies. The insurance giant Cigna faces a class-action suit in U.S. District Court in Connecticut over its billing practices, including for the filters, hoses, masks, and other supplies needed for CPAP machines—the continuous positive airway pressure devices sleep apnea patients use to keep their airway open at night. One of the plaintiffs, Jeffrey Neufeld, contended in the case that Cigna billed the cost of his supplies through a middleman who jacked up the prices.

Neufeld declined to speak to me, but his attorney, Robert Izard, told me Cigna contracted with a company called CareCentrix, which coordinated a network of device providers for the insurer. Neufeld decided to contact his provider directly to find out what it had been paid for his supplies and compare that with what he was being charged by CareCentrix. He discovered that he was paying CareCentrix substantially more than the device provider told him it was being paid by CareCentrix. For instance, Neufeld owed $25.68 for a disposable filter under his Cigna plan while the device provider said it was paid $7.50. Neufeld owed $147.78 for a face mask through his Cigna plan while the device provider said it was paid $95.

I looked up the CPAP supplies billed to Neufeld online and found them at even lower prices than those he said the device provider had been paid. Longtime CPAP users say it's well known that supplies are often cheaper when they are purchased without insurance.

Izard said the plaintiffs in the case contend that the cost "should have been based on the lower amount charged by the actual provider, not the marked-up bill from the middleman."

Patients covered by other insurance companies may have fallen victim to similar markups, he said.

Cigna would not talk to me about the case. But in documents filed in the suit, it denied misrepresenting costs or overcharging Neufeld. I called the device company to ask them about it, but they never called me back.

Stephen Wogen, CareCentrix's chief growth officer, would not talk to me, but he sent me a statement that is interesting. He said insurers may agree to pay higher prices for some services while negotiating lower prices for others, to achieve better overall value. For this reason, he said, isolating select prices doesn't reflect the overall value of the company's services. That's interesting because his statement seems to confirm that lower prices may be available without paying through your insurance plan. Apparently some patients enjoy the benefit of lower prices while others get penalized for using the insurance plan that's costing them monthly premiums. That's not reassuring.

It's not just happening with CPAP supplies. I talked to a mom who discovered the same type of scheme driving up the price of the baby formula she had been purchasing through her insurance plan. She had a high deductible and realized it would be much less expensive if she paid cash for the formula.

Do your own price check.

You don't have to be an insider to find out how you can pay less without insurance. My colleague at *ProPublica* teamed up with a reporter at the *New York Times* to see if they could get lower prices on commonly prescribed drugs without using their insurance plans. One reporter had pharmacy benefits through OptumRx, which is owned by UnitedHealth Group, the other through Express

Scripts. Those are two of the biggest players in the pharmacy benefits world. The reporters used GoodRx to identify one hundred commonly prescribed drugs and to check the prices.[7] GoodRx gathers prices for more than seventy thousand pharmacies in the United States. It's a good place to see whether you might be able to get a drug at a better price than what you're paying on your insurance plan. The two journalists found better prices on GoodRx for at least forty of the one hundred most prescribed drugs. That's incredible. Many of the drugs could be purchased without a coupon for $4 at Walmart, they found.[8]

In many cases the amount of the patient's copayment has been found to be higher than the actual price of the drug. Say you have a $10 copayment every time you pick up a particular drug at the pharmacy counter. That seems like a great deal. But what if it's a generic drug and the cash price is $3? You would still be required to pay the $10 and the extra money that comes in would go back to the insurance company—which is known as a clawback payment. Many states are passing laws prohibiting the practice, but it has been a standard way of doing business. A 2018 study found that almost a quarter of filled pharmacy prescriptions in 2013 involved a copayment higher than the average reimbursement paid by the insurer for that drug.[9] The clawbacks underscore the deceptive profiteering in American health care. There's little regard for what's fair to patients.

Try my price-check experiment with your health plan.

Talking to so many people about this phenomenon of saving money *without* insurance made me curious about my own health plan. My family's monthly insurance premiums are so high we have rich benefits—including a deductible of zero. But we still have copays and cost sharing. So typically, I would not think that it would be better for me to skip using my insurance for the care we receive.

I performed a quick experiment. I chose two common blood tests—the complete blood count, CPT code 85025, and the basic metabolic panel, CPT code 80048. I called an independent lab facility near my home in New Jersey and asked them how much I would pay for each blood test, first using my UnitedHealthcare insurance plan and second if I paid cash. The answer? The complete blood count would cost me $64 with insurance and $19.20 without. The basic metabolic panel would cost me $73 with insurance and $21.90 without.

How is that? I asked the guy on the phone. Without insurance they give a 70 percent discount, he explained, as if it made all the sense in the world. "Sometimes the deal with insurance is great, sometimes it's better to pay cash," he said matter-of-factly. "It's all up to you, sir."

TAKE ACTION

Always ask for the cash price. It might be a better deal than if you ran what you need through your insurance plan.

PART III

Employer Section

WE HAVE SEEN HOW INDIVIDUAL PATIENTS CAN SAVE hundreds or thousands of dollars on health care by putting insider knowledge into practice. The savings are magnified exponentially when it comes to employers.

If you're an employer, you may represent our greatest hope to bring about meaningful reform to the health care system. Employers are the sleeping giant of health care reform. They steer more than 150 million Americans to doctors, hospitals, insurance companies, and other medical providers. Employers have an untapped pipeline of power and influence because they control what the health care system needs to survive: money.

Right now, most employers don't seem to realize the health care industry is running what's akin to a con game on them to take that money.[1] Employers need to sponsor health benefits for their workers. Typically, they trust health insurers to wrangle the costs on their behalf, whether they're in a fully insured plan or self-fund their benefits and pay one of the big insurance carriers to administer the benefits. The typical employer trusts the façade that's created by the insurance carriers: *We care about lowering your health care costs. We advocate for you. We are giving you the best possible deal.* That trust is misplaced. They often don't realize that behind the scenes the industry is working against them. The health insurers team up with the medical providers and drug manufacturers to make the costs so difficult to understand that few employers feel equipped to hack through the thicket. So they don't.

In the following section, I've highlighted three focus points for any employers who want to pay less for health benefits while also providing good coverage for their employees. The first chapter in this section is focused on making sure the broker who is advising you is not in the pocket of the insurance companies or other vendors who may be trying to increase the cost of your health plan. The next chapter shows how one savvy plan administrator in Montana stopped paying ridiculously high prices compared with what Medicare pays, showing how you can, too. The final chapter in this section reveals how the insurance companies have made it embarrassingly easy for people to steal your health plan's money by committing fraud—which is driving up health care costs for all of us—and shows you how to identify the fraud and stop it.

I love to talk to the employers who have caught on to the game and flipped it on the health care players that have been taking advantage of them. I feature several of them in the coming chapters. They're like converts to an empowering and freeing way of thinking and behaving. They shake their heads at all the years that they were duped but refuse to mope about it. They're taking action and changing the way they provide health benefits for their employees, saving themselves and their workers money while improving their health coverage. There's a groundswell of these reformers across the country and we need others to follow their lead. They are fulfilling the audacious proposal I made at the beginning of this book: paying less for health care and getting more for their money.

9

The Conflict of Interest Undermining Employers' Purchase of Health Benefits

THE PITCHES TO THE health insurance brokers who advise employers would make anyone jealous.

"Set sail for Bermuda," said insurance giant Cigna, offering top-selling brokers five days at one of the island's luxury resorts.

The pitch from insurer Health Net of California was not subtle: a smiling woman in a business suit riding a giant $100 bill like it's a surfboard. "Sell more, enroll more, get paid more!" In some cases, its ad said, a broker can "power up" the bonus to $150,000 per employer group.

Not to be outdone, New York's EmblemHealth promised top-selling insurance brokers "the chance of a lifetime": going to bat against the retired legendary New York Yankees pitcher Mariano Rivera. In another offer, the company, which bills itself as one of the nation's largest nonprofit insurers, focused on cash: "The more subscribers you enroll . . . the bigger the payout." Bonuses, it says, top out at $100,000 per group, and "there's no limit to the number of bonuses you can earn."

Such incentives sound like typical business tactics until you understand who ends up paying for them: the employers who sign up with the insurers—and, of course, their employees.

Human resource directors and company executives and owners often rely on health insurance brokers to guide them through the tangle of costly and confusing benefit options offered by insurance companies. But what many don't fully realize is how the health insurance industry steers the process through lucrative financial incentives and commissions. Those enticements, critics say, don't reward brokers for finding their clients the most cost-effective options. They reward them for sticking with the same old thing.

Brokers provide a variety of important services to employers. They present them with benefit options, enroll them in plans, and help them with claims and payment issues. Insurance industry payments to brokers are not illegal and have been accepted as a cost of doing business for generations. But when brokers are paid directly by employers, the results can be mutually beneficial.

If you're an employer, whether you've got a few employees or hundreds or thousands, you should pay close attention to who is paying your broker or consultant and how much they are making by bringing your business to the insurer and other vendors. If your adviser is making an income from someone other than you, then ask yourself whether your adviser has the financial incentive to push back against the medical industry to do what's best for you and your employees. You may want to make a switch and pay the consultant yourself.

Fortunately, the Consolidated Appropriations Act, 2021, should make it easier than ever to quantify how much money brokers and consultants are making. After I wrote about this issue for *Pro-*

Publica in 2019, senators added it to a sweeping piece of health care legislation. Then it got added to the Appropriations Act, which was better known for providing COVID-19 relief checks.[1] The Act required brokers to disclose to employers any direct or indirect compensation that comes from industry vendors. It doesn't take away the conflict of interest, but at least it brings it out in the open. But you still need to pay attention and be on the lookout for the industry's influence.

See if your broker is guilty of a bui: "brokering under the influence" of industry cash.

Here's how it typically works: Insurers pay brokers a commission for the employers they sign up. That fee is usually a healthy 3 percent to 6 percent of the total premium. That could be about $50,000 a year on the premiums of a company with one hundred people, payable for as long as the plan is in place. That's $50,000 a year for a single client. And as the client pays more in premiums, the broker's commission increases.

Commissions can be even higher, up to 40 percent or 50 percent of the premium, on supplemental plans that employers can buy to cover employees' dental costs, cancer care, or long-term hospitalization.

Those commissions come from the insurers. But the cost is built into the premiums the employer and employees pay for the benefit plan.

Now, layer on top of that the additional bonuses that brokers can earn from some insurers. The offers, some marked CONFIDENTIAL, are easy to find on the websites of insurance companies and broker agencies. But many brokers say the bonuses are not disclosed to employers unless they ask. These bonuses, too, are indirectly included in the overall cost of health plans.

Here's the big question: How is it possible for brokers to independently represent what's best for the employers they advise when their paychecks are coming from the insurance carriers and other industry vendors?

Spoiler alert: It's not possible.

I ran these industry payments by Eric Campbell, director of research at the University of Colorado Center for Bioethics and Humanities. He told me they can't help but influence which plans brokers highlight for employers. "It's a classic conflict of interest," Campbell said.

Let's not pretend that insurance brokers are somehow immune to the influence of money. We know other professionals are not. Real estate agents were less likely to sell, or took longer to sell, residential properties listed with lower commissions, a team of researchers from Cornell, Massachusetts Institute of Technology, and the University of Pennsylvania showed.[2] Biased investment advice is a pervasive problem when financial advisers are conflicted, studies show.[3] In June 2019 the Securities and Exchange Commission adopted regulations requiring financial brokers to disclose to their clients any potential conflicts of interest.[4] Journalists are also vulnerable to the lure of gifts and money. In my twenty-year journalism career I have always worked for media outlets with strict conflict-of-interest policies that prohibit accepting any cash or gifts. I won't even let my sources buy me a cup of coffee.

Campbell pointed to the overwhelming evidence that shows how pharmaceutical money influences physicians. My *ProPublica* colleague showed that doctors who take money related to a specific drug are more likely to prescribe that medication than their colleagues who aren't financially tied to that drug.[5] Other research has shown that pharma industry payments to doctors increases the odds of their prescribing costly brand-name drugs.[6] There's "a large body of virtually irrefutable evidence," Campbell said, that shows drug company payments to doctors influence the way they prescribe. "Denying this effect is like denying that gravity exists." And there's no reason, he said, to think health benefit brokers are any different.

Brokers are a linchpin in the deals between insurance companies and the employers paying for health benefits. And yet experts told me there's been scant examination of their role in the marketplace. A Johns Hopkins team led by Dr. Marty Makary, my friend and collaborator, analyzed the commissions paid to brokers in 33,689 fully insured health plans and found a median commission of 4.1 percent of the premium each year. That's like buying a house and paying your agent a commission every year that you own it. Based on their findings, the average American worker will pay about $4,000 in earnings to a health insurance broker over the course of a career without even knowing it, Makary said. The study did not include the bonuses paid to brokers because those are not tracked in a way that's publicly reported. The commissions were found to be associated with the premiums, which, Makary said, suggests that the brokers could be influenced by a conflict of interest that's driving up costs. It could be beneficial to report the commission as a per member per month cost that's built into the health plan to increase transparency, the study suggested.[7]

Where evidence does exist about the influence of commissions, "it shows this is a problem," Daniel Schwarcz told me. Schwarcz is a law professor at the University of Minnesota who has studied the existing studies of insurance company payments to brokers in the property and casualty market. "You see good evidence that brokers and agents are not always giving advice that is directed toward improving the interests of policyholders," Schwarcz told me. "It's more directed toward maximizing commission."

When a health benefit broker is getting paid by insurance

carriers and other vendors, they may not be open to options that detach an employer from those same carriers and vendors. Critics say the setup is akin to a single real estate agent's representing both the buyer and the seller in a home sale. A buyer would not expect the seller's agent to negotiate the lowest price or highlight all the clauses and fine print that add unnecessary costs.

One of the most perverse problems is making the commission a percentage of the total premium. That means the broker makes more money when employers and their employees pay more. "If you want to draw a straight conclusion: It has been in the best interest of a broker, from a financial point of view, to keep that premium moving up," said Jeffrey Hogan, a regional manager in Connecticut for a national insurance brokerage and one of a band of outliers in the industry pushing for changes in the way brokers are paid.

Consult a broker who is not funded by the industry.

The more innovative insurance brokers now oppose these industry payments, even though it's been the standard way of doing business. As the average cost of employer-sponsored health insurance premiums has tripled in the past two decades, to more than $21,300 for a family, a small but growing contingent of brokers are questioning their role in the rise in costs. They've started negotiating flat fees paid directly by the employers. The fee may be a similar amount to the commission they could have earned, but because it doesn't come from the insurer, Hogan said, it "eliminates the conflict of interest" and frees brokers to consider unorthodox plans tailored to individual employers' needs. Any bonuses could also be paid directly by the employer.

Some brokers are taking both direct fees from employers and bonuses and commissions or other payments from insurers and other vendors. Others say all that's required is to disclose the payments they get from the other industry players to employers. But the cleanest arrangement for employers is to use a fee-only consultant—where the *only* money the broker makes is from the employer's direct payment. That way there's not even anything to disclose to the employer because there are no conflicts. The employer can be assured the consultant is working 100 percent on his or her behalf.

Palmer Johnson Power Systems, a heavy equipment distribution company in Wisconsin, switched to a reform-minded broker, David Contorno, and saved big on its health plan while also improving benefits for its employees. The company saved so much in 2017 that the owner rewarded employees by taking them on an all-expenses-paid trip to Colorado, where they rode four-wheelers and went whitewater rafting. In 2018 the company saved money again and rewarded each employee with a health care "dividend" bonus of about $700. In 2019 it continued its excellent performance. And in 2020, because of the COVID-19 pandemic, the plan greatly reduced its spending.

Contorno's company, E Powered Benefits, is based in North Carolina and Oregon but works with employers all over the country. Contorno is still getting paid for his services, but by the employers who are his clients, not the insurance companies or other vendors. Contorno takes a flat fee, plus a bonus based on how much the plan saved, and his total payments have worked out to what he would have made in the old days, when the insurance companies signed his paychecks.

Contorno began advising Palmer Johnson in 2016. When he took over, the company had a self-funded plan and its claims were reviewed by an administrator owned by its broker, Iowa-based Cottingham & Butler. Contorno brought in an independent claims administrator who closely scrutinized the claims and provided detailed cost information. The switch led to significant savings, said Craig Parsons, the company owner. "It opened our eyes to what a good claims review process can mean to us," he said.

Brad Plummer, senior vice president for employee benefits for Cottingham & Butler, acknowledged to me that "things didn't go swimmingly" with the claims company. But overall his company provided valuable service to Palmer Johnson, he said.

Parsons said he saw a big difference in the solutions provided by Contorno when he entered a direct-pay relationship. The new payment arrangement puts pressure on the broker to prevent overspending. His previous broker, he said, didn't have any real incentive to help him reduce costs. "We didn't have an advocate," he said. "We didn't have someone truly watching out for our best interests."

Contorno used to operate the traditional way. Back in 2011 he had been happy with the status quo: He had his favored insurers and could usually find traditional plans that appeared to fit his clients' needs. But he began to see that the health plans the carriers were offering created the same problems again and again for the employers and their employees. He started to understand that the big insurance companies didn't have any intention of driving down costs or giving employers a better deal. And it dawned on him that he was part of the problem. And now he regrets his role in driving up employers' health costs. One of his LinkedIn posts compared the employer's acceptance of control by insurance companies with Stockholm syndrome, the feelings of trust a hostage would have toward a captor. Now he says one of the biggest lies being sold to employers is that the only way to reduce costs is to cut benefits to employees. He has found that he can reduce costs while improving benefits.

Contorno also provided resources to help Palmer Johnson employees find high-quality, low-cost providers. The company had the Cigna network at the time, so prices were set by the carrier if employees stayed in network. But here's how wonky health care can be: They could often get better prices by going out of network. Contorno set them up with a vendor that had prenegotiated prices with a national network of doctors and surgery facilities and imaging centers.

Palmer Johnson waived employees' out-of-pocket costs if they chose to use the providers that had the set prices, saving the employee and the plan thousands or even tens of thousands of dollars, depending on the service or procedure.

Palmer Johnson also contracted with a vendor for drug coverage that does not use the secret rebates and hidden pricing schemes that are common in the industry. Palmer Johnson's yearly health care costs per employee dropped more than 25 percent, from about $11,252 in 2015 to $8,288 in 2018. It went a little higher in 2019, but then dropped to about $8,200 again in 2020. That's lower than they'd been in 2011, Contorno said.

Contorno no longer manages the Palmer Johnson benefits, because he had a noncompete agreement with the broker agency he worked with when he began working with them. But Palmer Johnson officials told me their plan is still doing well and saving money on benefits with the plan he helped put into place.

Ashley Matthys, director of human resources for Palmer Johnson, said a key to making the benefits work is ensuring that it's a partnership between the employees and the employer. The employees need to understand how the health care system works and how it affects how much they themselves pay out of their pockets. It also ensures they get quality health care for the money they spend, she said. "A lot of employers would say they don't have enough employees to take this on," Matthys said. "But we're small. You're never too small to start it."

Contorno now consults for about three dozen employers, ranging in size from about fifty employees to thousands. He co-brokers the benefits for a few dozen more. The employers in his stable have evolved beyond the traditional preferred provider organizations— better known as PPOs. The PPOs contractually prohibit employers from setting the price, because the carriers are contractually obligated to agree to the discounts or prices they've negotiated with their in-network doctors and medical facilities, Contorno explained. So now the benefits plans he manages do not have any network at all. It's a similar arrangement to the one Marilyn Bartlett put into place for Montana employees, which I describe in the following chapter. The plan sets its rates at 150 percent of Medicare rates for facilities and 140 percent for medical practitioners, Contorno said. So there are no in-network or out-of-network providers. There's no network.

The plans typically run smoothly, with no hassle. But sometimes a hospital or doctor will "balance bill" a patient—meaning they send the patient a bill for the balance of what the health plan would not pay. In those cases, the employer's benefits plan defends the patient—contesting the bill and enlisting an attorney to fight the case, if necessary. The worst-case scenario is agreeing to pay what the medical provider wants, which is the same discounted amount the employer would have been paying under a traditional PPO network. Except in that case, the employer would have been paying those PPO rates for every claim.

Breaking free of the insurance industry's bonuses and commissions has spurred Contorno to come up with better benefits arrangements for the employers he serves. He said it's completely different from the traditional arrangement, which keeps brokers subservient to the insurance carriers.

"Now that my compensation is fully tied to meeting the clients' goals, that is my sole objective," he told me. "Your broker works for whoever is cutting them the check."

Make sure your consultant works for you, not your insurer.

Contorno is part of a group called the Health Rosetta, which certifies consultants who agree to follow certain best practices related to health benefits, including eliminating any hidden agreements that raise the cost of employee benefits. To be certified, their benefits advisers must disclose all their direct and indirect sources of income—bonuses, commissions, consulting fees, for example—and who pays them to the employers they advise.

Dave Chase, a Washington businessman, created Rosetta in 2016 after working with tech health startups and launching Microsoft's services to the health industry. He said he saw an opportunity to transform the health care industry by changing the way employers buy benefits. He said brokers have the most underestimated role in the health care system. "The good ones are worth their weight in gold," Chase said. "But most of the benefit brokers are pitching themselves as buyers' agents, but they are paid like a seller's agent."

There are more than two hundred Rosetta-certified brokers, and many others who follow a similar philosophy consider themselves part of the movement. But the industry is large, with tens of thousands of brokers. So those committed to being paid directly by employers and being totally transparent about their income are challenging the status quo.

From the employer's point of view, one big advantage of working with brokers like those certified by Rosetta is transparency. The Appropriations Act now requires brokers to disclose their payments from the industry. But the Rosetta consultants who get paid by industry money have been sharing this information with their employer clients all along.

Industrywide, transparency has not been the standard. In 2019, I wanted to find out whether the largest broker companies had standards for what they disclose to employers about their commissions and bonuses from insurance companies. I sent a list of questions about the types of hidden compensation from the insurance industry to ten of the largest broker agencies, some worth $1 billion or more, including Marsh & McLennan, Aon, and Willis Towers Watson. Four firms declined to answer; the others never responded despite repeated requests. I have included a list of questions in Appendix C. It's a good starting point for employers, so they can have more constructive and informed conversations with their advisers about any potential conflicts of interest that should be factored into decision making.

The new Appropriations Act is going to be eye-opening for employers. Learning how much their brokers have been making from the industry vendors may be "the business equivalent of finding out your spouse was cheating on you," Chase said. Employers will rightly wonder why this information wasn't provided to them all along.

Chase said the next frontier is to reform the contracts that employers sign with the insurance companies and vendors that provide their benefits. They often limit an employer's ability to access the data they need to analyze their spending, or restrict an employer's ability to audit the claims, to make sure they are paid properly, as I cover later in this book. The industry's contractual norms have normalized deviant practices, Chase said.

I reached out to all the insurers I've named in this chapter and many didn't respond. Cigna said in a statement that it offers affordable, high-quality benefit plans and doesn't see a problem with providing incentives to brokers. Delta Dental emphasized in an email it follows applicable laws and regulations. And Horizon Blue Cross said it gives employers the option of how to pay brokers and discloses all compensation.

Some insurance company officials told me they always want a

broker to match employers with the best product for them, and that the bonuses and commissions do not create a conflict of interest for the brokers.

But some insurers' pitches, however, clearly reward brokers' devotion to them, not necessarily their employer clients. "To thank you for your loyalty to Humana, we want to extend our thanks with a bonus," says one brochure pitched to brokers online. Horizon Blue Cross Blue Shield of New Jersey offered brokers a bonus as "a way to express our appreciation for your support." Empire Blue Cross told brokers it would deliver new bonuses "for bringing in large group business . . . and for keeping it with us."

Delta Dental of California's pitches appear to go one step further, rewarding brokers as "key members of our Small Business Program team."

The effect of such financial incentives is troubling, said Michael Thompson, president of the National Alliance of Healthcare Purchaser Coalitions, which represents groups of employers who provide benefits to more than forty-five million Americans. He said brokers don't typically undermine their clients in a blatant way, but their own financial interests can create a "cozy relationship" that may make them wary of "stirring the pot."

Employers should know how their brokers are paid, but health care is complex, so they are often not even aware of what they should ask, Thompson told me. Employers rely on brokers to be a "trusted adviser," he added. "Sometimes that trust is warranted and sometimes it's not."

Brokers who have stopped taking insurance company money are uprooting the hidden ways the industry is taking employers' money. John Harvey, a Rosetta-certified Phoenix, Arizona, consultant, used to make his money the traditional way, through insurance company bonuses and commissions. He brought in so much money for insurance companies early in his career that they rewarded him with trips to the Super Bowl, Final Four, and golfing at Pebble Beach. Then he began to get uncomfortable with the lavish spending and what it meant to the employers and workers paying for the largesse. He started his own company, Wincline, and now makes money only from the fees paid directly to him by the employers he advises.

Being free of the insurance companies has made Harvey more motivated to dig into their schemes to save money for his employer clients. Those schemes include the hidden fees the insurers take when they administer self-funded plans. Here's how one of the common ones works. A self-funded health plan gets hit with a big out-of-network bill, and the insurer administering the plan negotiates a lower payment for the medical provider. Then the insurer pays itself a hefty fee based on how much it "saved" the health plan. And when I say it's a "hefty" fee, I mean it. I've pulled a lot of the agreements third-party administrators (TPAs) have with school districts and municipalities around the country. The fee taken by the administrator—typically one of the big insurance companies—for reducing the bill is often about 30 percent of the amount "saved." Think about how that incentivizes outrageous out-of-network bills. The bigger the billed charges, the bigger the discount, and the bigger the discount, the bigger the fee the insurer gets to pay itself from the employer's money.

Harvey has a great example that shows how crazy those fees can get. One of his clients' health plan got an out-of-network bill for $161,000 from an outpatient surgery center. The third-party administrator negotiated the payment down to $13,000. That sounds like a fantastic discount. But then the TPA rewarded itself with a $43,000 fee for the price reduction. That means the fee the TPA took to reduce the price amounted to three times what the medical provider received for the service. Harvey likes to say "right is right, wrong is wrong," and that he's "fired up" when he sees how the insurance industry cheats employers.[8] He said his advocacy for his employers is all possible because his payments come directly from the employers, not from the insurance carriers and vendors.

Make sure your broker isn't behaving badly.

Sometimes employers don't find out their broker didn't get them the best deal until they switch to a different consultant. Josh Butler, a Rosetta-certified broker in Amarillo, Texas, recalls taking on a company of about two hundred employees that had been signed up for a plan that had high out-of-pocket costs. The previous broker had enrolled the company in a supplemental plan that paid workers $1,000 if they were admitted to the hospital to help pay for uncovered costs. But Butler said the premiums for this coverage cost about $100,000 a year, and only nine employees had used it. That would make it much cheaper to pay for the benefit without insurance.

Butler suspects the previous broker encouraged the hospital benefits plan because it came with a sizable commission. He sells the same types of policies for the same insurer, so he knows the plan came with a 40 percent commission in the first year. That would mean about $40,000 of the employer's premium went into the broker's pocket.

Butler and other brokers said the insurance companies offer huge commissions to promote lucrative supplemental plans like dental, vision, and disability. The total commissions on a supplemental cancer plan one insurer offered came to 57 percent, Butler said.

These massive year-one commissions lead some unscrupulous brokers to "churn" their supplemental benefits, Butler said, convincing employers to jump between insurers every year for the same types of benefits. The insurers don't mind, Butler said, because the employers and employees end up paying the tab through their premiums. Brokers may also "product dump," he said, which means pushing employers to sign up employees for multiple types of voluntary supplemental coverage, which brings them a hefty commission on each product.

Build your own health benefits.

Carl Schuessler, a broker in Atlanta who is certified by the Rosetta group, said he likes to help employers in fully insured health plans find out how much profit insurers are making on their premiums. Some states require insurers to provide the information, so when he took over the account for The Gasparilla Inn, an island resort on the Gulf coast of Florida, he obtained the report for the company's recent three years of coverage with UnitedHealthcare. He learned that the insurer had paid out in claims only about 65 percent of what the inn had paid in premiums.[9]

But in those same years the insurer had increased the inn's premiums, said Glenn Price, its chief financial officer. "It's tough to swallow" increases to our premium when the insurer is making healthy profits, Price said. UnitedHealthcare declined to speak to me about the case.

Schuessler, whose company, Mitigate Partners, is based in Atlanta, said he tries to move employers from "insurer-built" to "employer-built" benefits. The inn had seen costs go up every year before he transitioned it to a self-funded plan.

Schuessler and other consultants say moving from a fully insured to a self-funded plan is the most important first step because it allows the employer to break free of the prepackaged plans offered by the insurance carriers. Traditional insurance is a black box that is loaded with hidden costs. There's no way to see a spending breakdown and impossible to weed out the lucrative industry self-dealing that makes insurance carriers some of the most profitable companies in the country. In the past, an organization would have to have more than two hundred employees before they would go into a self-funded benefits plan, where the employer takes on the burden of funding the costs. But now some consultants are helping organizations with fifty employees, and sometimes fewer, transition to a self-funded plan.

Typically, even self-funded employers are having their benefits administered by one of the large insurance carriers. Schuessler and other consultants who are helping employers pay less and get more say it's essential to break free of using the big carriers as third-party administrators—the ones who grant access to their networks and process the claims. The big carriers won't blink when they use a self-funded employer's money to pay one hospital $130,000 for a knee replacement and $40,000 at another, Schuessler said. He said Gasparilla once got a $20,000 bill for a colonoscopy! A good plan administrator will review outlandish costs, he said, or engage a vendor who will review them, and refuse to pay them.

With Gasparilla's new self-funded plan, the goal was to reduce the cost to the inn and its employees while improving the benefits. Deductibles for the two hundred employees dropped from $2,500 for individuals and $4,500 for families to zero. Copays on generics and many brand-name drugs were also eliminated.

The resort contracted for primary care at a clinic that's a few hundred yards away for $15 per visit. For emergency care, employees obviously don't have the option of choosing where to go. So the plan pays about 150 percent of what Medicare pays for emergency visits. For care that can be planned in advance, the inn has a custom-built network of medical providers, including doctors and hospitals that have agreed-upon rates. It's a direct-pay relationship that cuts out the hassle and bureaucracy of dealing with a large insurance carrier. The plan offers noncontracted providers a fee that's based on a percentage of Medicare. If a provider comes after the employee for more money, the plan has patient advocates on call to handle the bill. The inn still allows employees to go anywhere else they want for care, but the employee will pay a higher copay. That gives employees the incentive to go to the medical facilities and doctors who are contracted with the health plan.

Price said now he can see all the claims that the plan is paying. In the past, the big insurers refused to give him the data he needed to understand his company's spending, he said. In the first three years, the inn saved $1.8 million, or 34 percent, on its total spend. The company must be more hands-on to run the new plan, Price said, but it used some of the money it has saved to hire a person they call their benefits champion to focus on it.

Schuessler said the plan works because it saves a tremendous amount of money to eliminate all the middlemen who are unfairly tapping into what employers spend on health care. The doctors and hospitals appreciate getting paid directly by the health plan because they get paid quickly—without battling an insurance carrier—and there are no copays or coinsurance for the patients, which saves the medical provider the pain of chasing down a patient for payment.

Schuessler has packaged benefits into what he calls the Fair Cost Health Plan, so he can replicate the inn's success for other employers. DeSoto Memorial Hospital, a 315-employee facility in Arcadia, Florida, recently completed its first year on the plan. It went from spending $2.2 million in a traditional PPO model to $990,000 with direct contracting for medical services. That's a savings of $1.2 million—55 percent. Meanwhile, employees had no copays and no deductibles on the plan.

Schuessler and others also put a fair cost health plan in place in Florida for the school district of Osceola County. One of the solutions involved a company called Green Imaging, which contracts directly with imaging centers across the country to provide MRI, CT, and other scans at a reasonable price. The health plan waived out-of-pocket costs to members to incentivize them to use the Green Imaging centers. In the first year, the health plan saved 61 percent, about $1.5 million, on its imaging. That's a big savings that could be used for teacher salaries or school supplies. The cost of health benefits is drastically reduced when the middlemen are removed from the equation, Schuessler said.

Again—employers are finding that brokers who break free of the medical industry's payments are helping them fulfill my audacious proposal. They are paying less for their health benefits and delivering better care to their employees. It is possible. Employers merely need to stop being satisfied with the status quo.

TAKE ACTION

1. Ask your broker to disclose all sources of his or her income related to your employer-sponsored health plan. Your trusted adviser may be making bonuses and commissions from many more sources than you think. Health Rosetta requires its certified advisers to disclose *all* their sources of compensation to their employer clients. The organization has a form on its website that shows more than a dozen types of compensation: medical, prescriptions, dental, vision, stop loss, EAP, long- and short-term disability, cancer, wellness, and more.[10] Use the form as a model for your broker to sign.

2. If your broker is getting paid by insurance companies or other health care vendors for work associated with your health plan, then ask how you can be assured that the

broker is independently pushing back against the industry to get you the best benefits at the lowest price for your organization.

3. Ask your insurer to tell you how much of your organization's premiums are being spent on health care claims, like Schuessler does for his clients. He said insurers are required to provide the information in some states.

4. If your broker is taking industry money, then at least have a conversation with an adviser who is not feeding at the trough of insurers and other vendors. See if the consultant you can pay yourself can offer solutions that will save you and your employees money while delivering the same level of health care coverage.

10

The Buyer Sets the Price

WHEN MARILYN BARTLETT STARTED leading the health plan for the State of Montana's employees and their families, she faced a problem. The state's health plan, which covered about thirty thousand people, was in deep trouble and in desperate need of a fix. Losses were projected to top $50 million within several years. Bartlett was going to lead the charge to turn things around.

Bartlett knew employers have negotiating power that few of them use. The health care system depends on the revenue produced by their employees' surgeries, mammograms, lab tests, and other services provided under their plans. The medical providers can ill afford to lose access to the revenue brought in by employee health plans. She had a bold strategy. First: Tell the state's hospitals what the plan would pay. It would be a fair price. Take it or leave it.

Second: Demand a full accounting from the company managing drug costs. If it wouldn't reveal any side deals it had with drug makers, replace it. Rise up. Push back.

Bartlett would be taking on some of the state's power players: hospitals and health insurers—and their politically connected lobbyists. If her plan didn't work, the state and its employees were in trouble. If it did, the health plan would be saved from insolvency.

As you will see, her plan *did* work. It wasn't easy, but Bartlett created a blueprint for employers everywhere.[1] If you are an employer and you are reading this chapter, you may be able to apply the six steps below that Bartlett took to reduce her health plan's spending while delivering high-quality care for employees and their families.

Employers: *You* must address the problem of ballooning health care costs.

If you're an employer or work for your employer's benefits team, you may be wondering how you found yourself in this perplexing situation. Employer-sponsored health benefits are almost as old as America itself. In 1798 John Adams, the second U.S. president, signed a law that took 20 cents per month from the paychecks of U.S. seamen to fund their medical care. After the Civil War, lumber, mining, and railroad companies needed health care services as they blazed a trail across the American West. So they withheld money from employee paychecks to pay for doctors and hospitals.[2]

The modern insurance era can be pegged to the start of the Blue Cross plans, in 1929, with a plan for Dallas schoolteachers. The employer-based system became entrenched when wages were frozen during World War II. Employers couldn't lure the best workers by offering them higher pay, so they compensated them with more generous benefits. The carriers realized they could make big money in health insurance. So employer-sponsored health benefits went mainstream. Today, most American adults under age sixty-five get their benefits through their employer. The industry is dominated by the big insurers. Half a dozen of them sit near the top of the Fortune 500, with combined annual revenue of about half a trillion dollars.

Despite the money at stake, many employers have, wittingly or not, deferred to the industry. Decisions about health benefit plans are usually made by midlevel human resources managers, who may not understand the forces in the health care industry operating against them. They're often advised by insurance brokers, who are traditionally funded by the industry, as I pointed out in the previous chapter. And they're trying to keep the peace for employees who demand convenient access to the care they need. It's a recipe for inertia.

You probably wish someone else would handle this problem for you, but that's the problem. The conventional wisdom is that insurance companies want to reduce health care spending. In reality, insurers' business plans hinge on keeping hospitals and other providers happy—and in their networks—often at the expense of employers and workers. That means this is something you have to do yourself.

I talked to Michael Thompson, who leads the National Alliance of Healthcare Purchaser Coalitions, about the difficult dynamic faced by employers. Employers often feel caught between rising costs and concern that changes they make will be bad for their employees, Thompson told me. And, he says, they rely on the advice of industry experts instead of digging into the details themselves. But one thing is sure, he told me: Employers must fix the problem.

"We have got to get control of this thing or it's going to bring down the economy, our personal bankrolls, and our wages," he told me. "It'll cost jobs in the United States and it'll bring down our public programs. This is not a small issue. It's a huge issue."

Bartlett said employers need to ask more questions to force the health care industry to justify every dollar it spends, and they can't stop until they have the spending itemized and explained. As she discovered, it's not easy. The industry players are aligned with one another, not with their paying customers.

When she took over the Montana employee health plan, Bartlett quickly discovered that it was easier to talk about pushing back than to do it. But step by step she took on the challenge. Her success provides the playbook for other employers who need to do the same thing. Many are now building on her groundbreaking work.

STEP 1: You need to get ahold of your claims data.

Bartlett arrived in Helena, the state capital, in the fall of 2014 as an outsider navigating a minefield of established relationships. From the start, she knew she'd have to tackle the staggering bills from the state's hospitals, which made up the largest chunk of the plan's expenses. If a health plan can reduce hospital expenses, it can right the ship. It wouldn't be popular because they also made up a significant chunk of the hospitals' profits.

Montana, like most large employers, self-funds its plan. That means it pays the bills and hires an insurance company or other firm to process the claims. More than half of American workers are covered by self-funded plans. You would think employers would have the right to know what they're spending their money on. But remember—the health care system profits by hiding this information from the people paying the tab. Bartlett considered herself—on behalf of her health plan—the boss in her arrangement with Cigna, which managed the plans. She assumed she'd have access to detailed information about how much Montana's taxpayers and employees paid for procedures at each hospital. But when she asked Cigna for its pricing terms with the hospitals, Cigna refused to provide them.

Its contracts with hospitals were secret, Cigna representatives told her. That didn't sit well with her, Bartlett recalls. "The payer cannot see the contract," she says, "but we agree to pay whatever the contract says we will pay."

A cumbersome querying process set up by Cigna allowed her to get individual claims and other limited information. But the company would only give her aggregate data, with things lumped together, to show what her plan paid each hospital. I've talked to many self-funded employers who are having this same problem. This is like telling a family trying to reduce its total spending on utilities without providing an individual breakdown of what it spends on heat, air-conditioning, electricity, and water. It's hard to lower the total if you can't see which items might be needlessly driving it up.

When Bartlett continued to demand information, Cigna balked, saying it needed to balance what she wanted with keeping the hospitals happy. "I don't see the need for a balance," she recalls telling them. "I am representing the payer."

Cigna would not speak to me about its relationship with Montana's plan. The company would only send me a statement, saying it had prioritized the plan's preferences and needs.

STEP 2: Examine how much you're paying for individual claims.

Keep in mind that an entire ecosystem of vendors is making a nice profit on what you spend on your health plan. And in many cases their profits increase when your costs rise. They might not like it if you start asking how you can spend less for the same thing. Bartlett got fed up and ended the plan's relationship with Cigna.

Her battle to upend the status quo riled even some employees in her own office, who complained that she was demanding too many changes. Some quit. Bartlett didn't relent. That Christmas, the Cigna representative sent each employee in Bartlett's office a small gift, a snow globe. Bartlett didn't get one.

The plan signed on with a new administrator, Allegiance Benefit Plan Management, which is, ironically, a Cigna company. Finally, Bartlett could get an analysis of individual payments for health care services provided to the employees. When she saw the data broken down, she couldn't believe what it showed about the prices.

As I explain elsewhere in this book, hospitals typically charge a high price for a procedure, then give insurers in-network discounts. The insurers might have much different discounts for each procedure at each hospital, depending on who has more leverage during negotiations. Most people have no idea how big the variation is when it comes to paying for medication or medical services, although now the federal government does require hospitals to report these negotiated rates.

The insurance network discounts, however, are meaningless if the underlying charges aren't capped. When Bartlett looked at a common knee replacement, with no complications and a one-night hospital stay, she saw that one hospital had charged the plan $25,000, then applied a 7 percent discount. So the plan paid $23,250.

A different hospital gave a better discount, 10 percent, but on a sticker price of $115,000. So the plan got billed $103,500—more than four times the amount it paid the other hospital for the same operation. It would have paid that much, except Bartlett caught it and was able to reduce the payment to $60,000.

Bartlett recalled wondering why anyone would think this was okay. She wanted to know how a hospital could be paid so much for a knee replacement. But Allegiance wouldn't give her the information, citing its contract with the hospital. That didn't stop Bartlett. She found a work-around—going directly to the hospital to get the bills. She discovered that about $70,000 of the total charges were due to the cost of the implant. Bartlett knew the implant cost was ridiculous. But again, she had to find her own work-around to investigate. She tracked down the sales representative for the device company and learned the hospital had paid $3,500 for the device. She discovered that Montana taxpayers and employees were being asked to pay a 2,000 percent markup. Ouch. Standard economic models don't work when all the costs and prices are hidden from the funders. "They don't price their product at what the market can bear because the market has just followed wherever the hospitals take us," she told me.

If you're an employer, I obviously can't see your data. But I can almost guarantee your health plan is getting ripped off in a similar way. Your employees could be getting the same services for much less if they go to some facilities and avoid others. This is the standard way the industry operates. I have mentioned elsewhere in this book, like in the chapter on protecting yourself from price gouging, that employer-sponsored health plans are being overcharged all over the country. Researchers from the RAND Corporation compared what Medicare paid with what employers were paying hospitals. Employers were paying two to three times more than Medicare, on average, with no relationship between cost and quality.

The RAND researchers published a map that shows the higher- and lower-cost health care systems in each state.[3] Check the hospitals near you to see how they might have variation in pricing.

Bartlett took a similar approach to the RAND researchers. She had Allegiance compare what the plan was paying each hospital with what it paid Medicare. She discovered the plan paid hospitals, for the same services, anywhere from about twice to about five times the Medicare prices. In other words, if Medicare paid a hospital $10,000 for a particular procedure, the Montana plan would pay anywhere from $20,000 to $50,000 for the same thing. She knows how cost shifting works, so employers and their workers are expected to pay more than the government plans. This type of discrimination against workers is standard in American health care. It's come to be accepted, even though it's unjust. There's no reason employers and employees should be paying more for the same services a hospital will provide to a Medicare patient for much less. Bartlett could see that some of the hospital prices were over the top! She would need to get the high-priced hospitals to take something closer to what her plan paid the lower-priced hospitals.

STEP 3: You are the payer, so you set the price.

Before she got hired, Bartlett had explained a vision for establishing what the plan would be willing to pay for medical services. Medicare would be the reference point. Medicare adjusts its prices for hospitals based on geography and other factors. Hospitals complain that the Medicare rates are too low, but cost reports show that hospitals routinely profit on Medicare payments, Bartlett said. Also, hospitals need to reduce their spending. They're wasting resources and adding unnecessary administrative costs. The problem may not be that Medicare doesn't pay them enough. They just need to stop wasting money. Plus, perhaps the strongest argument for the adequacy of Medicare prices is that hospitals continue to accept and care for Medicare patients. Bartlett saw herself as the fiduciary for her health plan, which means she had a duty to protect the plan assets and manage them on behalf of the employees and taxpayers funding the benefits. Employers covered by the federal ERISA law are fiduciaries, so this is their duty, too.[4] So, Bartlett wondered, why would an employer-sponsored health plan be expected to pay so much more? That's what everyone who works in the world of employer-sponsored health plans should be asking.

Montana's plan determined it would pay hospitals a set percentage above the Medicare amount, a method known as reference-based pricing. That makes it impossible for the hospitals to arbitrarily raise their prices. It also protects employer-sponsored health plans from the secret game of inflated charges and discounted prices, which empowers the industry to extract more money than it deserves from health plans. The buyer sets the price.

No one wanted to stiff the hospitals, but these prices were ridiculous, Bartlett remembers thinking. She determined the new rate for all hospitals would be a little more than twice the Medicare rate—still a rich deal, but a good starting point to get prices under control. The contracts would also prohibit hospitals from billing patients for whatever charges a health plan refuses to pay, known as balance billing. And because every hospital in the state would be on board, all the state's employees would be in the network.

It would mean a boost in pay for some lower-cost hospitals. Now, she had to persuade the more expensive hospitals to take less.

STEP 4: When you're negotiating, don't blink.

If you're running a business, you routinely shop and negotiate and bargain to make sure you get the best deal on the resources you need to operate your organization. You should do the same thing with your health benefits.

Kirk Bodlovic, the chief operating officer of Providence St. Patrick Hospital in Missoula, remembers the day an entourage from the state health plan, including Bartlett, arrived at his hospital.

Bodlovic knew from Allegiance's reports that St. Patrick's prices were on the high side. But he wasn't prepared for the ultimatum: If St. Patrick's wanted to treat state employees, the hospital would have to accept lower rates. If it didn't, the state would pay for its employees to travel to other hospitals.

"You're in or you're out, basically," Bodlovic says.

There were thirteen hospitals that accounted for almost all of the state health plan's hospital expenses—and about four dozen smaller facilities in rural areas. Bartlett needed to get the big facilities on board, and it meant some of them would be taking a pay cut. Her plan had leverage because it's the largest in the state, but she had to be strategic. She started with the ones that charged the lowest prices. Once they signed on to the plan it would be easier to flip the higher-cost facilities.

The state's demand set off a series of meetings within the Providence chain, which also operates in California, Alaska, and the Northwest. It didn't have a lot of leverage because Missoula is a two-hospital town. Its competitor, one of the lower-priced facilities, had already agreed to the deal.

St. Patrick's considered rejecting the deal. Bodlovic told me that that thought gave him heartburn. He envisioned the wrath of doctors if some three thousand state plan members had ended up at a rival hospital. And the hospital would have lost about $4 million in annual revenue. "That's a good chunk of business," he says.

In their final analysis, he says, St. Patrick's officials decided it was the lesser pain to accept the new contract than to be left out of the deal.

While the state worked to get hospitals to sign new contracts, their CEOs and lobbyists plotted end runs, scheduling meetings with the governor's office to propose alternative solutions. When they arrived for the meetings, they found that Bartlett had also been invited. She effectively blocked their ideas. Bartlett said that other political allies also had to run interference. The health care industry is accustomed to getting its way when it comes to local and national politics. And it's not accustomed to employers demanding a fair deal.

Bartlett had to get all the hospitals on board—or else. The new pricing was set to go live on July 1, 2016, and, with a month to go, six of the major hospitals were holding out. "I started to panic," Bartlett recalls. During sleepless nights, Bartlett imagined thousands of state employees being forced to zigzag across the state for medical care or running up massive bills at noncontracted hospitals.

With her stomach in knots, she went on the offensive. She took a graph showing the variation in hospital prices to state legislators. Then she threatened to go public. She couldn't name names because of contract restrictions, but she could tell the media that some hospitals' prices were many times higher than others' and let journalists figure out which ones were which.

Five of the holdouts surrendered and signed the contract. "The hospitals didn't want that out there," she says.

Only Benefis Health System in Great Falls, one of the higher-priced hospitals, refused.

STEP 5: Enlist your allies.

The new plan went into place July 1, 2016, without Benefis as a contracted hospital. Bartlett ratcheted up the pressure one more time, calling in the Montana Federation of Public Employees. In the Great Falls area the union had hundreds of members, including Keith Leathers, who worked as an investigator with the state's child support enforcement division. Leathers has a young daughter with scoliosis, and he didn't want to drive long distances to get her the care she needs. He readily engaged in the fight.

"We have a regional medical facility here that's supposed to be able to handle almost any medical problem, period," he recalled thinking. "And I got to go out of town to get care because they want to charge more than anyone else?"

Union leaders launched a campaign against the hospital. Leathers says he sent a postcard and made a phone call every day to the hospital CEO, the board members—anyone he could find in leadership. He urged them to accept the new rates. Hundreds of other employees from across the state did the same.

Within a month, Benefis agreed to join the health plan. The hospital declined to speak to me about it.

Leathers says employers and workers should be protesting health care costs "over and over again" everywhere in the country. "Are we going to wait until the health care system just crashes?" he asks.

Most employers seem to be so afraid of making waves for their employees that they don't do anything to improve their health plan. Instead, they just pass the annual increases to the workers, which raises their premiums and out-of-pocket costs. But Bartlett showed the power of employers and their workers joining forces to pressure the medical industry to stop taking unreasonable amounts of their money. It worked in Montana and she says it could work in one form or another in other places, too. One example is Pacific Steel & Recycling, also located in Montana, which took a similar approach and reduced its annual health care spend by more than half, from $8 million to $3.5 million.[5]

If you're an employer, take the time to show your employees that it's their compensation getting consumed by rising health care costs. Your employees probably don't understand this because, as I showed in chapter one of this book, most employees don't see the connection between rising health care costs and their stagnant wages. They might not understand that every dollar wasted on overpriced or unnecessary health care is a dollar that can't be paid to them in salary. If your employees understood this, they might be more open to finding benefit solutions that will cost less and provide more.

When Bartlett took over the state health plan, it spent about $200 million a year. Bartlett's team estimated that the new hospital pricing schedule saved the plan more than $17 million in the second half of 2016 and all of 2017—almost $1 million a month. By 2017 a plan that state officials had predicted would go broke had turned itself around. By late 2017 the plan had so much in reserves it stopped taking premiums from the state coffers and put about $25 million back into the state's general fund. The plan has continued to have excess reserves.

STEP 6: Uproot hidden drug spending.

Bartlett had one more target in her sights: prescription drug costs.

Health plans contract with separate companies, middlemen entities known as pharmacy benefit managers, to get members their medication. And everyone assured Bartlett the state's pharmacy benefits deal was state of the art. But just as with Cigna, she insisted on examining it herself. That wasn't easy because the pharmacy benefits were run through a cooperative arrangement with other health plans, including those of universities, school trusts, and counties. The state plan anchored the co-op, and the other partners were happy with the arrangement.

Bartlett knew that pharmacy benefit managers are notorious for including deals that boost their profits at the expense of employers. One of the common tricks is a deceptive practice called the spread. A pharmacy benefit manager, for example, will tell an employer it cost $100 to fill a prescription that actually cost $60, allowing the pharmacy benefit manager to pocket the extra $40. The fine print in the contract often allows it.

The spread has been extensive. A recent report by the Ohio state auditor noted that the spread on generic drugs had cost that state's Medicaid plan $208 million in a single year—31 percent of what it spent.[6] In Kentucky, they found PBMs making $123 million in 2018 from spread pricing in the state's Medicaid program.[7] Michigan's Medicaid program got overcharged by an estimated $64 million in a two-year period due to spread pricing.[8] The Pharmacists Society of the State of New York reported in 2019 that the state's Medicaid program was overcharged by at least $300 million in this manner.[9]

Sure enough, when Bartlett got her PBM contract, she found that the state plan had fallen victim to the spread.

If you're an employer, or work on your employer's benefits team, ask your broker or consultant whether spread pricing is also baked into your pharmacy benefits. Remember, as I pointed out in the previous chapter, your broker or consultant might be getting paid a kickback by the pharmacy benefit manager that's used by your health plan. So the person who is supposed to be your adviser may not be as forthcoming as you would like. If that's the case, find an adviser who's not accepting industry cash who can give you some straight answers about the design of your pharmacy benefits.

Pharmacy benefit managers also rake in dollars through other hidden schemes, including rebates paid by pharmaceutical companies. Most health plans would assume that since they're paying for the drugs, they should get any rebates. But pharmacy benefit managers often don't disclose the size of the rebate, which allows them to keep some or most of it for themselves. When Bartlett pressed, she discovered the state wasn't getting the full amount of its rebates.

Montana was getting taken, but it put Bartlett in a touchy political situation. The co-op needed the state as a partner or it wouldn't survive. Bartlett decided her allegiance was to the plan's bottom line. She pulled out of the deal.

"She wasn't afraid of ruining her career or making people angry," one of the consultants who helped analyze the pharmacy benefit contract told me.

Bartlett says it helped that she was near the end of her career and didn't need to please people. "I'm sixty-seven, so I could give a shit," she told me. "What are they going to do, fire me? I'm packin' a Medicare card."

Bartlett found a pharmacy benefit manager, Navitus Health Solutions, that would not take any spread and would pass along all rebates in full. The next year, the plan saved an average of almost $16 per prescription. It purchased a similar mix and volume of drugs in 2016 and 2017. But it saved $2 million on the spread. And its revenue from rebates jumped from $3.5 million to $7 million, Bartlett said.

Beyond Montana

So how are Montana's hospitals after the price cut? Just fine, it appears.

Bob Olsen, vice president of the Montana Hospital Association, told me he did not hear hospital leaders say they are struggling under the new state contract. They have had "reasonable financial performance," he says.

The health insurance industry hasn't appreciated Bartlett's efforts. America's Health Insurance Plans, the lobbying group better known as AHIP, has been circulating propaganda that claims the changes to the Montana health plan didn't work. But AHIP is manipulating the facts, Bartlett said. For example, the AHIP document says the plan lost $2.8 million in 2018, but didn't consider that it saved so much it reduced premiums by $25 million. The

AHIP propaganda also claims the plan lost money on high-dollar cases, but those losses were mostly due to out-of-state cases that don't fall under the reference-based pricing plan, Bartlett said. The counterattacks are not a surprise, Bartlett said. The insurers haven't kept costs down and have profited by making employers spend more, she explained. Also, reference-based pricing eliminates their networks, which are a primary method of controlling the pricing and making them money. If employers set the prices—and thereby see the prices—insurers and hospitals can't continue profiting from exorbitant payments. "AHIP is feeling very threatened," she told me. "They're losing control."

To Bartlett, confrontation with the health care industry is something employers should expect. The industry players aren't going to smile when employers push them to justify their costs. But the more employers realize the industry's tricks and tactics, the more they will be emboldened to do the right thing and demand fair prices—or the industry risks them setting the prices themselves. The change has to start at the local level in each community, she said.

"You have got to step up," she said, imploring other employers to stop being bullied.

Bartlett's legacy may be even greater than her work in Montana. Her mission accomplished, Bartlett left her position as administrator of the state employee health plan. She went on to work for the Office of the Montana State Auditor, where she continued to take on pharmacy benefit managers. She is now a senior policy fellow at the National Academy for State Health Policy, where she is showing other state leaders how to protect themselves from the health care industry's profiteering. A new tool she developed helps self-funded employers analyze Medicare cost reports so they can see how much hospitals are making from Medicare payments.

That knowledge can give the employers the confidence to demand prices that are closer to the Medicare benchmark.[10]

Bartlett has testified before Congress and spoken at gatherings across the country. Her work has inspired other states and health plans, but not always with immediate success. North Carolina officials have been fighting for reference-based pricing in their state's employee benefits plan. One survey by an insurance brokerage firm found that about 2 percent of employers are in some type of a reference-based pricing plan, and another 10 percent are considering it. Many of the employers have been successful, but others have had to defend against doctors or hospitals sending balance bills to patients for whatever amount the plan refuses to cover.

Bartlett has also been working with employers by advising health plans in Colorado, Indiana, Maine, and other states. Colorado, where I grew up, has some of the highest health care prices in the country, despite its healthy population.[11] Go figure. Now, with Bartlett's help, employers in the state have laid the foundation to get a better deal from the health care industry.

"American employers cannot afford the corporate practice of medicine," said Robert Smith, executive director of the Colorado Business Group on Health.

Smith is part of a group that's formed the Colorado Purchasing Alliance,[12] to enter direct contracts with medical providers at fair prices. They're cutting out the middlemen who negotiate prices in secret, so doctors and hospitals can get a fair rate and the employers can avoid the markup.

Employers need to take the management of their health plans out of the hands of the human resources department and put it under the control of the C-suite, Smith said. Executives need to have the same diligence about purchasing health care that they apply to their purchase of other goods and services, Smith said.

They need to realize that the health care system isn't going to change without a fight. "It should come as a surprise to no one that everyone involved is trying to make as much money as they can," he said. "They're not going to give it up."

Incredibly, Bartlett accomplished what I call my audacious proposal. She found a way for state employees in Montana to spend less and get better care. If you're an employer, she says you should do the same thing. Bartlett has become a cult hero to the cadre of reformers who are taking on the health care industry. Her advice boils down to spurring employers to push back against the industry. "You've got to get in there and do it," she says.

TAKE ACTION

Smaller employers will need to work with a savvy consultant to take the steps that Bartlett put into place, and it will be a multiyear process. Larger employers or government health plans may have people in-house who have the expertise but may also want to consult Bartlett or other guides like her. But here are the steps they can take:

1. Get ahold of your claims data and find out how much you are paying for individual procedures and other services. Identify the least expensive and most expensive medical providers.

2. Compare what you're paying with the Medicare rates that the medical providers are accepting. Offer something higher than Medicare but lower than what you're currently spending. Employers who don't want to try to set their own rates can try to steer employees to the lower-priced hospitals. Use the map and downloadable data from the RAND Corporation to see which health care sys-

tems in your state are charging the most for medical care. See if your local hospitals are complying with the federal government's requirement for hospitals to post their negotiated prices with insurance companies. Remember, you are the payer, so you set the price. And if you can't set it, at least steer patients to the places with the best prices.[13]

3. When you're negotiating, don't blink. It's going to take backbone to stand up to the medical industry. They've been taking your money for years without your asking for a better deal. Expect the conflict and keep pressing.

4. Enlist your allies. Team up with other local employers to take on the health care players in your community. Get your workers on board. Communicate to employees what's being done to protect their compensation from getting sucked away by the medical system. Ask them to help you protect their compensation and wages by pressuring the medical providers to comply with your suggested rates.

5. Uproot hidden rebates and the spread in your pharmacy benefits. Again, this will take expertise, but find out if there are any hidden ways your money is being taken by your pharmacy benefit manager.

6. If you're an employee, consider asking your employer whether they are aware of the various ways the medical industry is raking in its profits. Remember to be cautious when you talk to your human resources department, because they might feel criticized by your questions or feel like you're blaming them for high health care costs. You may get a better response going to your chief financial officer or chief executive officer, if you have access to them.

11

Check Your Receipts. You Might Be a Victim of Fraud.

I N MAY 2020 Dr. Zachary Sussman went to Physicians Premier ER, a freestanding emergency room in Austin, Texas, for a COVID-19 antibody test. He assumed they'd give him a test for free. After all, Sussman, who is a pathologist, was then working part-time for the chain, supervising the tests. And he knew that the materials for the tests cost only about $8. Everything seemed okay when he did the test, which turned out negative. But weeks later he saw that the facility had charged his insurance plan $10,984. Even more astonishing—his insurance plan paid it in full!

Sussman felt so spooked by the charges and payment he resigned from his job. "I have decided I can no longer ethically provide Medical directorship services to the company," he wrote in his July 13 resignation email. "If not outright fraudulent, these charges are at least exorbitant and seek to take advantage of payers in the midst of the COVID19 pandemic."

Sussman called his insurer, Golden Rule Insurance Company, and reported the payment to a fraud investigator. He walked the investigator through each line of the charges and explained that many of the charges were linked to services that were never provided. The fraud investigator gave it a shrug, Sussman said. "His attitude was kind of passive," Sussman said. "There was no indignation. He took it in stride, like, 'Yep, that's what happens.'" The investigator said he would escalate the case to see if the facility had submitted any other suspect claims. But Sussman never heard back about his report of suspected fraud.

I wrote about Sussman's experience for *ProPublica*.[1] USA Emergency Centers, which owns the facility, denied doing anything wrong. I contacted UnitedHealthcare, which owns Golden Rule, and they said they would review the payment. Sussman said he later received an explanation of benefits that showed the money had been repaid.

For all their talk about protecting health care dollars and fighting fraud, insurance companies have shown themselves to be easy marks. In Sussman's case it might have been a mistaken payment, price gouging, or it could have been attempted fraud. But no one seemed to take him seriously when he reported it. That's not uncommon. I've done extensive digging into the problem of improper payments and health care fraud and found there is little meaningful enforcement in the world of employer-sponsored health benefits. Employers and workers need to closely examine their claims data and explanation of benefits documents to make sure they aren't getting ripped off.

I've already described some of the reasons our health care costs are so high—including overtreatment and high prices. But reducing fraud might be the most obvious way we could all start saving money. In 2019 private insurance spending hit $1.2 trillion, according to the federal government, yet no one tracks how much is lost to fraud.[2] Some investigators and health care experts estimate that fraud eats up 10 percent of all health care spending, and they know schemes abound.

Most people assume their insurance companies are tightly keeping watch over their health care dollars. Insurers themselves boast of this on their websites. But here's an unsettling reality about the nation's health insurance system: It is surprisingly easy for fraudsters to gain entry, and it is shockingly difficult to persuade insurance companies to stop them. And while we see headlines about the authorities busting people for fraud in the taxpayer-funded government Medicare and Medicaid plans, prosecution for fraud against employer-sponsored health plans is rare. We are all paying for it.

Your insurance company is probably not protecting your health care dollars.

If you're a self-funded employer, do not underestimate the incompetence of the insurance companies you trust to make sure your health plan doesn't get taken by fraudsters.

Consider how UnitedHealthcare got bamboozled and handed money that belonged to Southwest Airlines to a criminal. The airlines' flight attendants rejoiced when they learned their health benefits plan would cover their workout sessions. It might have sounded too good to be true, but sure enough, when they went to David Williams, a personal trainer based in Fort Worth, Texas, he and his team of trainers ran them through their weight training and cardio and billed their insurance plan, which was administered by United. The flight attendants flocked to Williams and referred their family and friends. He built up a network of personal trainers, who worked in several states. It seemed like such a great deal—until it became clear that it wasn't.

The Southwest Airlines benefits plan did not cover personal fitness. But Williams, who had a criminal record, had discovered massive loopholes in the integrity of our health care payment system and was running a crude but effective fraud. He didn't have any credentials but called himself a medical doctor and applied for the number medical providers need to bill insurance plans—the national provider identifier number, better known in the industry as an NPI. The federal government administers the NPIs through its Medicare program and, as Williams demonstrated, hands the numbers out to anyone who applies, whether or not they are an actual medical provider. Even though health care fraud is an epidemic, Medicare doesn't take the time to verify the accuracy of the applications. That means any criminal can get an NPI in a few minutes online. Then they can start billing insurance companies.[3]

United also didn't check whether Williams was a medical doctor, even though he was billing for care that can be provided only by a doctor. Insurance companies use computers to autopay almost all the claims that get submitted, so Williams simply sent in claims and cashed the checks. Sometimes the claims he submitted were for actual workouts. But other times they were not. Southwest wasn't the only company getting bilked. Other employers who had their benefits managed by Aetna and Cigna were also losing their money to the scheme.

Early in the fraud, Williams's ex-wife and her father caught on to his fraud scheme and started notifying the insurers by calling their fraud departments. But even then the insurers continued paying the claims. Williams kept ahead of the carriers by creating new NPI numbers—at least twenty in all—so he could continue getting paid.

By the time the authorities stopped Williams, he had been running the scam for more than four years, fraudulently billing

United, Aetna, and Cigna for $25 million and reaping about $4 million in cash. Southwest Airlines was the biggest loser. United paid out more than $2 million in fraudulent payments from the airline's self-funded benefits plan. The airline declined to talk to me about the case.

Williams got prosecuted for the crime and a jury found him guilty in 2018. He now sits in a federal prison. I reached out to him and he responded with a brief handwritten letter. He didn't deny billing the insurers and defended his work, calling it an "unprecedented and beneficial opportunity to help many people."

"My objective was to create a system of preventative medicine," he wrote. Because of his work, he claimed, "hundreds of patients" got off their prescription medication and avoided surgery.

The success of Williams's spree lays bare the financial incentives that drive the system: Policing criminals eats away at profits for the insurance companies. Ultimately, fraud losses are passed on to their clients through higher premiums and out-of-pocket fees or reduced coverage. I have talked to more than a dozen fraud investigators who worked for insurance companies as well as federal prosecutors who have taken on health care fraud. They all told me the same thing: The private health insurance carriers are not effectively tackling the problem of fraud. Insurers "are more focused on their bottom line than ferreting out bad actors," said Michael Elliott, former lead attorney for the Medicare Fraud Strike Force in North Texas.

Private health insurers allow so much fraud that prosecutors use an idiom to describe the rare person who gets caught: "Pigs get fat, hogs get slaughtered."

"Pigs" can steal millions if they bill just enough to avoid notice. But if they get greedy and bill too many millions, they "become a data outlier," Elliott told me. "You get slaughtered."

Of course, this isn't the way the carriers promote themselves when they bring in employers as their clients. They promote themselves as guardians of health care dollars. The insurance carriers also claim to have sophisticated fraud analytics capabilities. But Williams used his actual name and address and phone number when he submitted his bills. And his fraud went on for years after they knew about it. Somehow the carriers kept paying and paying and paying.

Part of the problem, experts say, is that health care fraud is often misunderstood as shafting greedy insurers—not the folks paying for health insurance or benefits. But ultimately, as I explained earlier in this book, this is our money, not theirs. If you're running a self-funded plan, then, obviously, the only money that's getting lost is yours.

You need to check the receipts.

The rampant fraud in employer-sponsored health plans—and the failure of insurance carriers to stop it—has tremendous implications for all the employers and workers paying high health care costs. It underscores the need for employers and anyone covered by their plans—all of us—to be vigilant when it comes to ferreting out fraud. We need to check the receipts.

When I was a kid my mom would cart me along with her to the grocery store. I'd always get a free cherry chip cookie from the bakery and then beg for a pack of Bubble Yum in the checkout line. And then I'd notice how my mom would scrutinize the ribbon of receipt that got spit out of the cash register, to make sure there hadn't been an error that led to her overpaying for any of the items. This is something all of us need to do whenever we undergo medical treatment, or order a medical device, or get prescribed a drug. We need to check the receipts!

As I explain in chapter two, one of the main "receipts" our

insurance carrier provides to patients is the explanation of benefits. A typical EOB will include the date of the service, the name of the doctor or hospital or other facility, the type of service, and the name of the procedure or test or device. I've described EOBs and how to read them in chapter two. It's essential that you verify that these things were billed accurately because you are the one who knows what services you or your loved one received. Your insurance carrier and employer do not have insight into what happened. They can see only what the medical provider claims happened.

The EOB may also list the codes that were used to bill your insurance plan. If it doesn't, request them. The type of code depends on the type of care you received. I go into more detail about codes in chapter two, but medical providers bill with current procedural terminology, or CPT, codes. Hospitals use international classification of diseases, or ICD-10-PCS, codes for the procedures they bill. All of those codes are easy to look up online, and they should also include a description of what type of service is expected with each code. Looking up the codes can reveal one of the most common types of fraud—upcoding—in which a medical provider exaggerates the complexity of whatever services are provided to get paid more for the visit. In the case of Williams, his favorite billing code was 99215, which is supposed to be used rarely because it requires a comprehensive examination and high level of medical decision making. He used that same code to bill United for more than $20.5 million in services—without apparently triggering any red flags with the insurer. But a patient who went to one of his training sessions might be able to tell that doing jumping jacks and weight training doesn't qualify as a medically complex service. You might also be surprised to discover charges on your EOB for services that were never provided.

If you're running a self-funded employer plan you also need to check your receipts. Be wary of putting blind trust in your insurance companies or other third parties that administer your health plan. There is a good chance your money is not being adequately protected from fraud. You can ensure the integrity of payments being made under your health plan by getting ahold of the data that shows how much you're paying for each claim, with the underlying medical codes that justify each claim. You can analyze the payments yourself, with some practice, or hire one of the many vendors who are experts in ferreting out fraud in employee health plans. I've spoken to the experts at ClaimInformatics and Scott Haas at USI Insurance Services and they provide these types of services.[4] These types of experts will likely pay for themselves by identifying the money lost to fraud and improper payments and by helping the employer to recover it.

It may seem like a lot of work as a patient to compare your medical bills and EOBs with the treatment you received. But this is your money being taken. Some employers give their employees the incentive to identify errors in their medical bills by letting them share in the money the health plan saves by not paying for the errors. That's the type of reward that will make employees scour their bills for mistakes!

It may also seem like a pain as an employer to monitor how your organization's money is being spent. But you and your employees are the ones who are best positioned to catch anything suspicious. You also have the greatest incentive to identify and put a halt to the fraud. It may also seem unfair that we would have to check this stuff in the first place. Isn't this what our insurance carriers are supposed to be doing? Yes—but they're not doing it the way they should be, and it's costing you money. If you don't check the receipts your money could be flowing right into the hands of fraudsters.

Your health insurer is probably soft even when it catches someone committing fraud.

The Williams case highlights how easy the insurance companies are on the criminals who are stealing from employee health plans. Even after several complaints that directly pointed the insurers to the fraud, the mammoth health insurers reacted with slothlike urgency. Their correspondence, which I pulled from the court records, shows an almost palpable disinterest in taking decisive action—even while acknowledging Williams was fraudulently billing them.

Aetna wrote Williams in January 2015 to say it had reviewed his claims and found he wasn't a licensed doctor, resulting in an overpayment of $337,933. The letter said there appeared to be "abusive billing" that gave "rise to a reasonable suspicion of fraud." But the insurer also gave him a month to provide documentation to dispute the assessment. When Williams hadn't responded in three months, an Aetna investigator wrote to Williams's attorney, saying, "We are willing to discuss an amicable resolution of this matter," and gave him two more weeks to respond.

That August, an Aetna attorney sent Williams's attorney another letter, noting that Williams had submitted "fraudulent claims" and had continued to submit bills "even after his billing misconduct was identified."

In January 2016—a year after Aetna first contacted him—Williams agreed to a settlement that required him to refund the company $240,000 "without admission of fault or liability by either party."

But that didn't stop, or even appear to slow, Williams. Not only did he renege on that promise, he also picked one of his other NPI numbers and continued to file claims, resulting in another $300,000 in payments from Aetna. In total, Aetna paid Williams more than $608,000.

I asked Aetna about this. In emails, Ethan Slavin, a company spokesman, didn't explain why Aetna settled with Williams instead of pursuing criminal prosecution. He blamed the insurer's slow response on the lengthy settlement process and Williams's tactic of billing under different organizations and tax identification numbers. Williams did repay some of the money before defaulting, Slavin said.

United, one of the largest companies in the country, paid out the most to Williams. The insurer brought in $257 billion in 2020 and has a subsidiary, Optum, devoted to digging out fraud, even for other insurers. But that prowess is not reflected in its dealings with Williams.

In September 2015 United wrote to Williams, noting his lack of a doctor's license and the resulting wrongful payments, totaling $636,637. But then the insurer added a baffling condition: If Williams didn't respond, United would pay itself back out of his "future payments." So while demanding repayment because Williams was not a doctor, the company warned it would dock future claims he would be making as a doctor. That's absurd.

Williams responded a month later, noting that he had a Ph.D. in kinesiology and did rehab, so he met the qualifications of a sports medicine doctor.

United responded in November 2015 with the same argument: He wasn't licensed and thus needed to repay the money, again warning that if he didn't, United would "initiate repayment by offsetting future payments."

Williams took United up on its offer. "Please offset future payments until the requested refund amount is met," he responded.

Then Williams turned to another NPI number, records show, and continued submitting claims to United.

In January 2016 Williams agreed to settle with United and repay $630,000 in monthly installments of $10,000. Inexplicably, the agreement refers to Williams as "a provider of medical services or products licensed as appropriate under the laws of the state of TX" and notes that the settlement doesn't terminate his continued participation in United's programs.

Also in 2016 Williams obtained a new batch of NPI numbers from Medicare. As usual, he used his real name, address, and credentials on the applications. The additional numbers allowed him to continue to send claims for payment to United.

In November 2016 United investigators caught Williams again—twice. They sent two letters accusing him of filing 820 claims between May 2016 and August 2016 and demanded repayment. Again, almost inconceivably, the company threatened to cover his debt with "future payments."

In December 2016 United notified Williams that he had repaid only $90,000 of the initial $630,000 he owed and was in default. The following month, United told him he had to pay the remaining $540,000 within twenty days or he could face legal action. Williams replied, saying he wanted to renegotiate the settlement, but the insurer declined. Late that month, United said its inappropriate payments to Williams had ballooned to more than $2.3 million.

A United spokeswoman said it was difficult to stop Williams because he used variations on his name and different organizations to perpetrate the fraud. "He did everything he could not to get caught," Maria Gordon-Shydlo said.

But that's making it sound like Williams was a criminal mastermind. The truth is the insurers just didn't check to see if he was a doctor before they paid bills for services supposedly provided by a doctor. And then they didn't verify that the complex medical procedures described in the claims actually took place.

The United spokeswoman defended the response of the company, saying it had eventually referred Williams to law enforcement.

In all, United paid Williams more than $3.2 million—most of it after the insurer had caught him in the act. But in reality, the losses weren't all United's. Most of the fraud was funded by the employee compensation that belonged to its client, Southwest Airlines.

"It's just not worth it" for your insurer to ferret out fraud.

Many health care experts and fraud investigators said they weren't surprised to hear that insurers were slow to stop even such an outlandish case of fraud.

"It's just not worth it to them," said Dr. Eric Bricker, an internist who founded and spent years running a company that advised employers about their health benefits. For insurance behemoths pulling in billions, or hundreds of billions, in revenue, fraud that sucks away mere millions is not even a rounding error, he said.

And perhaps counterintuitively, insurance companies are loath to offend physicians and hospitals in their all-important networks—even those accused of wrongdoing, many experts have said. They attract new clients by providing access to their networks.

This ambivalence toward fraud, Bricker and others said, is no secret. Scammers like Williams are "emblematic of gazillions of people doing variants of the same thing," Bricker said. Insurers embolden them by using a catch-and-release approach to fraud, in which the insurers identify criminals, then let them go.

Fraud investigators who have worked for the big insurance carriers tell me the insurers don't police fraud as much as they could because it's expensive. It's hard for them to prove criminal intent as opposed to an honest mistake. Or maybe a doctor will claim to be doing some novel medical treatment that's in a gray area. One investigator who had worked with three major insurers said the amount of fraud was so great that they ignored suspicious cases worth less than $300, because it would cost more to investigate than they could recover. But like the case of Williams, those small cases add up. He billed in increments of less than $300 and it added up to $25 million.

One insider I spoke to worked as an attorney for United and advised its fraud unit for more than a decade. She believes fraudsters know they are less likely to be prosecuted by private plans. Billing data showed that people cheating United on the commercial side played it straight with Medicare, said the attorney who left United in 2014 and stressed that she is not speaking on its behalf.

If a doctor fleeces Medicare, the agency can block that person from billing it—a crushing blow. "We don't have the hammer on the private side or the commercial side that Medicare does," she told me.

Joe Christensen has pursued fraud for both government and commercial insurers, serving as a director in Aetna's special investigations unit, a team of more than one hundred people ferreting out fraud, from 2013 to 2018, and as the director of Utah's insurance fraud division for thirteen years. Fraud in government programs, like Medicare and Medicaid, gets more publicity, he said, and has dedicated arms of agencies pursuing fraudsters. But the losses may be even greater in the commercial market because the dollar levels are higher, he said.

Some commercial insurers take a passive approach, Christensen said, in part because it's expensive to press a fraud case. At Aetna, he said, investigators would identify cases of apparent fraud, but it was up to the executives and the legal team to decide how to handle them. Taking fraudsters to civil or criminal court requires resources, so the company often settled for trying to get repaid through settlements or blocking a suspect provider from billing, he said.

Christensen said while he was at Aetna, investigators almost never sought to partner with law enforcement agencies to pursue criminal cases. In 2018 he became the SIU director for a Southern California–based Medicaid plan called L.A. Care Health Plan, where he was allowed to take a proactive approach. In just about a year, he said, his much smaller team began thirty-seven criminal investigations with law enforcement agencies issuing search warrants and making arrests. Christensen moved on to a job with an insurer in Utah, where his family lives, so he could be closer to them.

I asked Aetna how many criminal cases it had pursued in 2017 and 2018. A company official said the question could not be answered because it does not track such cases. That's an interesting response. If they cared about fraud wouldn't they at least keep track of the cases?

Your health insurer is probably not pursuing criminal prosecution for fraud.

It seems to me that if health insurers really cared about stopping fraud they would do whatever they could to make sure fraudsters were prosecuted for the crime. We don't let bad guys break into people's homes and steal their money. So why would we let doctors and hospitals or people posing as medical professionals steal the money we're spending on health care?

I decided to see how often the health insurance companies even refer cases for prosecution. I couldn't examine the entire nation, so I focused on California, which is known for sunshine, surf, and health care scams. Suspicious billing and kickbacks are so common that there's a Medicare fraud strike force at its ground zero for schemes, Los Angeles. The state's Medicaid fraud control unit is also among the busiest in the country. All the fraud investigators I spoke to told me fraud may be even more common in employer-sponsored plans, because they pay so much more than the government programs. So naturally, the health insurers in the Golden State must also be nabbing plenty of people committing fraud, right?

Wrong. I called the district attorneys' offices in California's fourteen largest counties, which cover about 80 percent of the state's population, about thirty-two million people. These are the people who would get fraud cases referred to them by the insurance companies. I asked the prosecutors: "How often did a fraud case referred by a commercial health insurer lead to criminal charges in 2017 and 2018?"[5]

Several of them simply burst out laughing. The insurers do little to help prosecute fraud, the prosecutors said, "even though this is their company that's getting ripped off," one told me.

So how often had a referral from an insurer led to charges getting filed? Just 22 times total in the two years I asked about in those 14 counties. In comparison, the state's Medicaid fraud unit filed criminal charges for fraud against 321 medical providers in that time period. It also had 65 civil settlements and judgments and recovered more than $93 million.

The insurers do not seem to be "on the same page" with the prosecutors when it comes to protecting the integrity of the payment system, one of the prosecutors told me.

I wondered if the health insurers might be more willing to help out state regulators. In most states they're required by law to report cases where there's a "reasonable belief" that there's been fraud. So if their crack units are really on this problem there should be lots of reports, right? Wrong.

Michael Marben told me the health insurers in his state may be breaking the law. Marben is the director of the Commerce Fraud Bureau in Minnesota and said his office depends on reports from health insurers to identify trends and warn other insurers. But in 2017 all the insurers in the state referred just two cases of suspected fraud to his office. The next year they submitted only five. Those are the totals for all the companies combined!

It's not that everyone is "Minnesota nice" up north. In the same time frame the state's Medicaid fraud unit conducted 596 investigations and netted 134 indictments. In the auto insurance market, the Minnesota fraud bureau had more than 2,200 referrals, and most of them came from insurers, Marben told me.

There's "conscious underreporting" of fraud by the health insurers, Marben told me. "You can't have a company that doesn't experience fraud."

So what are employers supposed to do? Employers in fully insured plans may not be able to do much—other than consider going to a self-funded model where they can get more insight into how their health care dollars are being spent.

Self-funded employers, those who fund their employees' benefits, could do a lot more than most of them are doing now to protect themselves from fraud. It would be difficult for them to identify whether fraud actually occurred. But they don't need to prove fraud. What they need to do is identify suspicious overpayments that were approved by the company administering their health plan. That's actually quite easy, if they can get ahold of their claims data—which is their right to have, given they are the ones paying the bills.

The administrators running New Jersey's School Employees' Health Benefits Program could see their plan was being exploited when they analyzed their out-of-network payments to acupuncturists, chiropractors, and physical therapists. Their plan had virtually no limits for these payments, and it created a feeding frenzy of clinics trying to lure in as many teachers as possible for treatment.

One practice delivered bagels and orange juice to local schools. Another provided catered lunches and free chair-side massages on-site at local schools. The acupuncturists, chiropractors, and physical therapists donated cash, supplies, and even wheelchairs to local schools and districts. The leaders administering the health plan, which covered about 158,000 educators and their loved ones, could see that the plan needed to be redesigned. By their estimates the plan overpaid for the services by about $130 million a year. Imagine how many more teachers could be put in classrooms for that kind of money!

I obtained the claims payments made to these out-of-network providers through a public records request, as well as internal reports that showed how the money was being wasted. I wrote a story for *ProPublica* that showed how these medical providers were cashing in because of the poor design of the plan.[6] I found that some acupuncturists and physical therapy sessions were paid at more than $600 per visit, on average. More than seventy of them earned more than $200,000 in 2018 from the teacher plan alone, the data showed. The services of one acupuncturist, in that one year, brought in more than $1 million! It may not have been fraudulent, but it certainly showed exorbitant payments. The teacher unions were blocking the redesign of the plan, but then my story exposed the way taxpayers and teachers were getting ripped off by the out-of-network providers. They revised the plan design to limit the payments—which is estimated to save taxpayers that cool $130 million a year going forward. It also brought down premiums, which attracted more members to the plan.

Employers may also want to enlist experts who specialize in analyzing claims for overpayment and fraud. This service is provided by a lot of companies with the expertise to tackle the challenge, and they can pay for themselves by preventing a health plan's money from being squandered.

If someone tapped into your bank account and withdrew money and your bank did nothing about it, you would sound the alarm. That's similar to what's happening here, but it's happening because your health insurer or plan administrator is not protecting the money you pay for coverage. Then, the following year, you are expected to pay higher premiums and deductibles. You're always going to be the one to pay up, and it will continue until we make it stop.

TAKE ACTION

Dr. Eric Bricker, who has helped thousands of employers manage their benefits, said cleaning up fraud should be every health plan's number one priority. It's a way health plans can save big money, he said, without requiring any behavior change on the part of employees or medical providers. Here are Bricker's recommendations for employers:

1. Self-funded employers, get ahold of your data because you are the ones paying the bills. You need to know how many claims you paid to each doctor or hospital and how much each medical provider charged or was paid for each visit.

2. Analyze the high-volume providers, even if the amount charged or paid for each claim is low. Check the out-of-network and in-network providers.

3. Sort the data by the number of claims for each provider so you can see which providers have the highest number of claims. Look for little-known providers, he said. The largest hospital in your town will be high volume, but perhaps there's an off-the-beaten-path doctor or clinic or facility that has hundreds of claims within a calendar year, at a

high dollar charge per claim. It's easy for individual providers to rack up half a million in claims, he said.

4. Divide the number of claims by 260—the number of working days in a year. Is there a lesser-known provider that is seeing many of your employees per day? If so, that may be suspicious. If the volume for any one provider is especially high it may be possible the provider is waiving the out-of-pocket costs from your patients. If that's happening, it's fraudulent and can be stopped.

5. Alert the carrier managing your plan. Also, alert the state department of insurance. Both of those agencies may be too bureaucratic to take action, but be the squeaky wheel.

6. If the fraud is happening out of network, move to a point-of-service plan, also known as a POS plan, that doesn't pay out-of-network claims.

7. If you can, move the plan to a third-party administrator that has lower thresholds to examine individual claims. The major carriers might have auto-adjudication levels of $2,000 a claim or higher, meaning they don't even look at claims for lower amounts. But with a smaller TPA, they might examine any claim less than $500. Then suspicious claims can be caught before they get paid.

8. Work with a company that ferrets out the fraud, waste, and abuse in health care plans. These experts can identify where overpayments are occurring and help an employer recoup what's been overspent.

Individual patients can also check their receipts to be on the lookout for fraud. Employers may want to incentivize them to ferret out fraud by letting them share the savings when they discover a payment that should not be made.

1. Monitor your explanation of benefits to see whether they match the treatment or service that was provided. If anything shows up on an EOB that didn't happen in reality, it should be reported to the employer's health benefits department and also to the company that's managing the benefits plan. Refuse to pay any deductible or coinsurance or fee that's related to the care that did not transpire.

2. Demand an itemized bill that details the charges, including the billing codes, for each drug or procedure or treatment that took place. Then the bill should be scrutinized to make sure it reflects what actually took place.

3. Be suspicious if a medical provider ever offers to waive or reduce a copay or coinsurance payment or offers other enticements. That may be a sign that the medical provider wants to make an excessive charge to the health plan and needs the patient to allow it to happen.

Standing Up to Bullies

WHEN I WAS A WIMPY seventh grader at Bell Jr. High School in Golden, Colorado, in the 1980s, there was a Neanderthal of an eighth grader who would lumber around the playground looking for kids to terrorize. He was known for a particularly unsanitary method of bullying: He put his victim in a headlock and spat on his head.

One day at lunch I was standing out by the tennis courts with my buddy just minding my own business and this knuckle dragger came ambling over. He started his ritual with me: pushing me, calling me names, asking me if I wanted to fight. I didn't resist because I didn't want to fight—I just wanted him to go away. He didn't go away. As was his habit, he went for the finishing move. He put me in a headlock and hocked a loogie into my hair. I had to run to the bathroom and stick my head in the sink to wash it out.

The next day the bully was back. It happened again. Predictably. He pushed me, called me names, and asked if I wanted to fight him. I assured him I did not want to fight and you can predict the outcome. Again, the finishing move: headlock, hock, spit. And the cleanup: bathroom sink, wiping paper towels on my head, slinking back to class hoping no one noticed.

The following day rolled around and, you guessed it, here came the bully. But this time something awakened inside me. He started the dance, calling me names and pushing me, but something snapped in my mind. I interrupted the ritual and drew near to him.

"I don't care if you beat me up," I announced to his face. "I don't care if you show your friends and everyone else that you can beat up a seventh grader. You can show everyone how weak I am and how strong you are. If that's what you want to do, then do it. Beat me up. But *DO NOT* spit on my head."

I winced and braced myself, expecting him to lay into me. But I felt nothing but the breeze against my face. He turned around and walked away. He lost interest. And I realized a lesson I have carried with me for the rest of my life. A bully will keep pushing you around until you stand up to him. And sometimes, even though you're weaker, you can stand up to the bully and win. We deploy a powerful moral force when we stick up for ourselves when we're being wronged.

There's a reason so many movies feature scenes of weaker people standing up to bullies. Maybe you never had a bully spit on your head, but we can all relate in one way or another. It's deeply satisfying to see the victim prevail over the bully and to see the bully slinking away, humiliated, while the victim is celebrated as the victor.

This book is all about standing up to the bullies in the health care system. You have been bullied for so long that it's become accepted as normal by the policy makers and power players in the health care industry. They think it's okay to hide prices from you even though they know you can't afford to pay the bills. They tolerate the middlemen and markups that drive up costs because often *they are* the middlemen doing the markups! They don't care if your bills contain errors that drive up the costs. They just expect you to hand over the money and will send bill collectors after you if you don't pay up. Your insurance company has been profiting handsomely and expects you to continue playing by the rules it has created that work in its favor, not yours, even though you're the one paying the premiums. Everyone expects you to keep paying more money than you should just because that's how they make their money and that's the way it's always been.

I've heard powerful people in health care say patients won't ever be able to put into practice the types of steps I've recommended in this book. I know many employers have been passive in the past. And yes, it's true that some of these battles are confusing and take a good bit of tenacity. And some of them can't be won. But I think these health care insiders who profit from the status quo do not understand just how many times you and I have had the health care system spit on our heads. At some point, you have to say "Enough is enough" and tell the bully he has pushed you too far. Now it's time for him to back off.

I believe we are all at that point. And I know that if even a fraction of the people being bullied fight back—remember, more than 150 million Americans would fall into that category—then together we are a formidable force. We will not win every battle. But we will lose every battle that we refuse to fight, and we have nothing to lose by fighting. Even in the worst-case scenario, we end up paying what we would have paid without the fight but stick up for ourselves in the process.

This book does not capture every method you can use to take

on the health care system and win. But I hope it provides enough examples and the right mindset so you can develop your own tactics to fight back and win. Remember—it's already happening. Lots of people are standing up to this bully and making him walk away. They're saving hundreds or thousands of dollars in the process and empowering themselves, which is priceless. As I said at the beginning of this book, I want to hear your victory stories and share them with others. See my website, marshallallen.com, for more resources and to get in touch with me. We can continue the fight together. As I hope you can see, I take great delight in helping you take on the bully and win.

Acknowledgments

I am grateful to God for giving me the privilege of sharing this work with you. Special thanks go to my wife, Sonja, who has been my biggest supporter and a constant source of encouragement. She's borne the burden of all the hours I've been working on this book with grace and love. Our sons, Isaac, Ashton, and Cody, have been an inspiration. You guys are fine young men and I can't wait to see how you'll leave your mark on the world. My mom and dad make a brief appearance in this book, but I feel their presence throughout because of the positive influence they've had on me. And, Mom, I loved how you had my back with your diligent copy edits!

Thank you to Farley Chase, my literary agent, for believing in me and this project. Bria Sandford, my editor at Penguin Random House, came up with the smart how-to angle for the book and kept me from getting too wonky with it. I appreciate her investing in me. Many editors over the years have helped me improve as a writer and reporter. But I must give a shout-out to Tracy Weber, who guided me through so many of the *ProPublica* stories that made their way into this book. Chris San Juan and Christian Acker, from Mythic Proportions, have been a tremendous help with my branding and marketing. And thank you to the friends, experts, and thought leaders who took my calls to spitball ideas or provide feedback on drafts. They include: Dr. Eric Bricker, Dave Chase, Caroline Chen, Elbert Chu, Drew Dyck, Brian Eggleston, and Dr. Marty Makary, among others.

I would have nothing to write without the health care industry insiders who tip me off and help me understand the system. Thank you. I am honored by the individual patients who are bold enough to let me investigate and share their stories. Thank you for trusting me and serving the public.

Appendix A

Jeffrey Fox Describes How He Took on UCLA Health and Won

UCLA Health Overbilling and Open-Price Contracts
October 1, 2017
Jeffrey Fox

BACKGROUND

In October 2014, during a routine checkup, our primary care physician, part of the UCLA network that is in our insurance company's network, referred my wife to take our three-year-old son to their radiology office for a potential problem. She called the number given and made an appointment. They arrived at the appointment, and the scan was performed. The appointment took about 15 minutes. Nothing was discussed about charges before or after, since all our bills from UCLA had been reasonable for many years.

UCLA Health billed our insurance $2,448 for that appointment. This was $1,192 for ultrasound of the scrotum with Doppler, and $930 for duplex of abdomen/pelvic vessels, plus $326 for the physician to review the results. The insurance company discounted the total amount to $1,992.25 and paid $293.55, leaving us with a balance due to UCLA Health of $1,444.37 for the procedure, plus $254.33 for the doctors, totaling $1,698.70.

Upon receiving this information, I called UCLA Health to advise them that the $1,444.37 was not valid, and the $293.55 received from insurance was more than enough for the procedure. I told them I was going to pay the $254.33 for the doctors, which I did. No one acknowledged my concerns, and they stopped returning my calls. I then wrote a letter, dated December 23, 2014.

Representatives of the billing office replied by letter, dated January 27, 2015, offering only intransigence and misdirection. They told me on the phone, also, that it would represent insurance fraud if they were not to collect the patient's responsibility, so their hands were tied. This was a lie; I contacted my insurance company, and they told me UCLA Health was perfectly welcome to resubmit the claim for a lower amount. They also told me the government of California publishes a chart showing standard billing. I found this online, and it did show what they billed. But this proves my claim that they knew I was in the dark about pricing, and they meant for it to be this way. I only found this in a giant chart buried in a government website, and they should know that most of their patients wouldn't know about this. This document isn't a substitute for fair dealing with ordinary people seeking medical services.

At risk of losing my money, but in order to remove the leverage UCLA Health might have to damage my credit rating, I went to their office on February 20, 2015, and asked to pay the $1,444.37 due. The manager himself took my payment, and, thinking this dispute was over, displayed great relief in his body language as he handed me the credit card receipt and confirmed that it had been processed, until I handed him a letter demanding a refund. He refused to sign my copy to acknowledge receipt, and stormed out of the room.

When the billing office continued to completely ignore me as I followed up on my refund, I filed suit in small claims court. My filing included a plaintiff's statement that I brought to the hearing, making the open-price contract argument I discovered from comments on a law-related blog from Dr. Christopher T. Robertson.

FAIR PRICE RESEARCH

UCLA Health had billed small amounts for X-rays in the past, from $125 to around $200. It was reasonable to think an ultrasound in the same office would be about the same, not many multiples more.

UCLA has an office that provides cash quotes for services. I called them multiple times and got different quotes. I made sure to describe everything: ultrasound scrotum evaluation with Doppler. Once I was told $180, then another time $475, both including interpretation. A little while later, I called the radiology office directly, who didn't refer me to the cash quotes office but told me that it's $180, including physician's interpretation. This not only indicates the market value of their services is much lower than what I was billed, it shows they are not even set up to give an accurate price quote when asked.

Cedars Sinai offered $360 cash, including physician's interpretation. The Healthcare Bluebook showed $518 in our zip code for the closest services I could find, including physician's interpretation.

LEGAL ARGUMENTS

The open-price contract argument was easily winnable. But one thing I worried about was making this argument on a bill that was paid; I had found a case where a company lost due to having paid a disputed bill already. However, in that case, it was recurring billing, and the company paid the bill for several months before complaining. I also worried in general about having a court award money in a demand for a refund.

RESULTS

No one showed up on behalf of UCLA Health on the court hearing date. Of course, in small claims court as anywhere, to get a default judgment still requires you to show your claim has merit. The judge read only the filing forms, but did not take my plaintiff's statement. He briefly tested my open-price argument and the voluntary payment issue. He asked if we had asked about the price before receiving the service or signed anything agreeing to a price, and I told him we did not. I had claimed in my written filing that I made my payment under duress, to head off any voluntary payment defense. The judge asked how I indicated to them that my payment was under duress. I told him that I couldn't write this on a check or anything, since I paid by credit card, but that I had objected to the payment immediately after making it, so it's not like UCLA could claim some sort of hardship for having relied on this money. I also stated that the letter threatening to send me to collections on a bill that had been under dispute from the beginning should be sufficient evidence of duress.

The judge accepted these arguments, and awarded me the total amount of $1,698.70 that I had paid, plus the $293.55 paid by my insurance company, less the highest fair price I had found of $518 (as I had offered, honorably giving UCLA the benefit of the doubt). So my judgment was $1,474.25, plus court costs.

UCLA Health, being disorganized and having contempt in general for their patients, ignored my requests for payment, until

I threatened to have sheriff's deputies come and confiscate their computers to sell at auction, after which they sent a check via FedEx.

In the end, the whole process was satisfying. The moment I pulled the EOB out of its envelope that showed what we owed for this procedure, I told my wife we're not paying it because it's not fair, and within seven months I had total victory. I was fortunate that this was a small enough amount that I could pay it and pursue recovery, and to have the knowledge to execute a small claims court filing and service of process.

Thankfully, the $518 ultrasound showed no pathology that required treatment, and my son's symptoms went away, long before the billing issue was resolved!

December 23, 2014

UCLA Health
10920 Wilshire Blvd., Ste. 1600
Los Angeles, CA 90024-6502

Attn: Hospital Services Billing Dept.

Re: Guarantor Number:
      Account No.:
      Date of Service: October 24, 2014
      Statement Date: November 27, 2014

Dear Sir or Madam:

This is to advise you that the above-referenced billing is not valid. I request that you reverse the billing, and cease and reverse any collection activities and/or credit reporting you have done or are planning.

I have attempted to resolve this matter by phone, but only spoke to intransigent representatives of your billing office, who eventually referred me to M██ L████. I have left messages for Mr. L████ but he has not returned my calls after nearly two weeks. Therefore, I am sending this letter with an explanation of why your bill is wrong, and a clear course of action you can take to resolve this matter.

Here is the problem with your bill:

1. The amount charged is not reasonable. For a 15 minute appointment on a common piece of equipment, UCLA Health billed a total of $2,448, which includes your bill for Hospital Services, and a separate bill from Physician Services.
2. The amount charged is not customary in relation to the charges we have paid for other services at UCLA Health.
3. The amount charged is five to ten times the market rate in this geographic area, so it is not a customary or reasonable charge in any case.

I recognize that your business has a right, in general, to ask for more than the market rate for services you offer. However, your charges in this case are not valid because we had no mutual agreement on the price beforehand, and it is your fault we didn't.

UCLA Health
Attn: Hospital Services Billing Dept.

Re: Guarantor Number:
       Account No.:
       Date of Service: October 24, 2014
       Statement Date: November 27, 2014

December 23, 2014
Page Two

If you feel you are entitled to charge such high fees through some special intangible qualities your hospital or your ultrasound machine possess, any reasonable person would expect to be notified in advance. In other words, someone somewhere in your organization should have notified my wife, at any time after the order for the test was received, when she called for the appointment, or when she showed up for the appointment, that you wished to charge so much more for the services than what you know a regular customer of UCLA Health would expect to pay. There is no fee schedule posted in your office, and your staff at the clinic do not provide pricing information. Your silence on this issue conveys a message that you intended to charge an amount commensurate with the usual charges we have paid for similar services. A half-hour visit with a UCLA Health physician is billed at $230. We recently got an X-ray for which UCLA Health billed about $118. Therefore, a 15-minute ultrasound should be in that range.

Because it is perfectly reasonable for us to assume that your charges for this service will be similar to what you charge for other services, it is your responsibility to inform us in advance if you wish to charge an unreasonable price, and you did not. Therefore, our implied agreement is that the fees will be reasonable and customary.

At this point, you have already received $293.55 from my insurance company, which is more than the market rate for this service in this geographical area. Also, I and/or my insurance company will pay the amount of $254.33 billed for the radiologist's services through Physician Services billing. The total of $547.88 is way more than enough. I therefore demand that you credit the balance of $1,444.37 on this account, and close the account as having been paid in full.

Please contact me promptly on this to advise me what you intend to do.

Jeffrey Fox
(310)

Appendix B

Sample Letter to Send to a Health Care Provider Before Taking Them to Small Claims Court

Lisa Berry Blackstock, the patient advocate I featured in my chapter about how to sue to get what's yours, provided this sample outline of the letter patients should send to any health care provider before taking them to small claims court.

The letter should be sent via certified mail so there is a record that the medical provider received it. Again, you may need this later in your court case. Include the USPS tracking number.

Type or print clearly the body of your letter and make a copy for your files. The letter should include:

> Patient's (sender's) name, address, contact information in header, centered.
> Health care provider's mailing address; best to send to the attention of the billing department and copy the health care provider's general counsel, CEO, and/or CFO.
> Date of letter.
> Add a note—"Regarding Patient (Name) with Account number and date of service."

Dear _____,

After several attempts made in good faith to satisfy my $_____
bill with _____ (insert name of health care
entity) for a fair and customary price, the refusal of your
organization to respond in good faith leaves me with no
choice but to pursue this matter in small claims court in the
(city) _____, (county) _____,
and state of _____.

_____ county in the state of _____
provides me with the legal right to file two different claims,
each up to the amount of $_____, each to
argue and prove in the presence of a state judge that the
chargemaster price list employed by your health care facility
is unfair and inflated and seeks to take advantage of patients
and their loved ones who find themselves in vulnerable and
compromised situations.

(Health care facility name) _____ is
attempting to collect $_____ from me/my loved
one for (specify the care provided) _____.
After studying my medical records and corresponding itemized
bill(s) from your facility, in line with healthcarebluebook.com
(OR SIMILAR RESOURCE like FairHealthConsumer.org) I again
offer you—for the last time—a fair and customary lump sum
payment of $_____ to satisfy my financial
obligation in full for account number _____.

In the event that my last, best offer is not accepted by
(specify date; within fifteen to twenty days from the date of
this letter) _____, you can expect me to proceed with
small claims filing. You can expect to receive your summons
as defendant via a county deputy or summons service
professional.

It is my sincerest hope that escalation of this matter can be avoided. I appreciate your attention to this pressing situation.

Sincerely yours,

_____ (Name of sender)

Appendix C

_____

Sample Questions Employers Can Ask Their
Health Insurance Brokers and Vendors

Here are the questions I asked the largest health benefits broker companies in the country when I wrote about this issue for *Pro-Publica*. None of them would answer them for me. If you're an employer, that should raise your eyebrows. Ask your broker these questions so they can determine how money from the industry might be influencing their advice. Brokers can easily ignore my questions and feel like they can get away with it. But they better not ignore yours.

1. Do you or your company get paid any commissions from insurance companies or other vendors based on my organization's health benefits? (Yes or no)
2. Do you or your company get paid bonuses from health insurance companies or other vendors based on my organization's health benefits? (Yes or no)
3. Do you or your company receive any trips, meals, gifts, or other perks from health insurance companies or other vendors related to my organization's health benefits? (Yes or no)

4. Do you or your company get paid bonuses and/or commissions from health insurance companies or other vendors based on the loss ratio (or the profitability of the plan for the insurer) of my organization's health benefits? (Yes or no)

5. Do you or your company get paid bonuses and/or commissions from health insurance companies or other vendors based on the overall volume (including all business or new business) of employer-sponsored health plan members or groups? (Yes or no)

6. Do you or your company get paid bonuses and/or commissions from health insurance companies or other vendors based on the retention of employer-sponsored health plan members or groups? (Yes or no)

7. Do you or your company ever participate in "no shop" or "no market" offers on behalf of insurers or other vendors in which a bonus or commission is contingent on your not shopping an employer's benefits to other insurers or vendors? (Yes or no)

8. Do you or your company ever participate in vacations or trips or meals or other perks provided by insurance companies or other vendors, based on the volume or retention of employer-sponsored groups? (Yes or no)

9. Do you and your company *always* disclose *all* bonus and commission money, and any other trips, meals, or perks, to each employer group whose business might have qualified your company for the money or the perks? (Yes or no)

10. Do you or your agency participate in fee-only payment agreements in which the *only* income you receive is coming directly from the employer who is purchasing the health benefits? (Yes or no)

11. Do you or your agency participate in any payment arrangements in which the employer pays you directly for health ben-

efits *and* your broker or agency takes a commission or a bonus from the insurance company or other vendor? (Yes or no)

12. If you said yes to number 11: Do you *always* tell the employers who are paying you directly that an insurance company or other vendor is also paying you a bonus, commission, or other perk that's based on that employer's benefits? (Yes or no)

13. If you do take direct payments from employers, what percentage of your benefit revenue is fee based and what percentage is commission or bonus based? Ethics experts say it creates a conflict of interest for brokers to claim to represent the interests of employers and then get paid by the health insurance industry. Will you please provide your perspective to explain why you represent employers who are purchasing health benefits but then also get paid by the health insurance companies?

Notes

Introduction

1. It's important to obtain medical billing codes and look them up online to see what services they describe. It's easy: Get the code and go online to Google or another search engine and input the number plus the term "billing code." Check to see if the code that was used accurately depicts the services the patient received. I go into more detail about this in chapter two.

2. An AARP study found that more than half of U.S. households had no emergency savings account and about a fourth of families that bring in less than $40,000 a year skipped some type of medical treatment in 2018. Catherine S. Harvey, "Unlocking the Potential of Emergency Savings Accounts," AARP Public Policy Institute, October 2019, https://www.aarp.org/content/dam/aarp/ppi/2019/10/unlocking-potential-emergency-savings-accounts.doi.10.26419ppi.00084.001.pdf, accessed February 7, 2020.

3. The Federal Reserve found that about 40 percent of Americans could not pay off an unexpected bill of $400 or more without putting it on a credit card, borrowing from family or friends, selling possessions, or taking out a payday loan. "Report on the Economic Well-Being of U.S. Households in 2018–May 2019," Federal Reserve, https://www.federalreserve.gov/publications/2019-economic-well-being-of-us

-households-in-2018-dealing-with-unexpected-expenses.htm, accessed February 7, 2020.

4. The medical industry's conventional message is that rising health care costs are as inevitable as the rising of the sun. As if there's nothing we can do about it. The industry's thinking is so upside down that insiders, even some reformers, call it a win when they *slow the increase* in spending. But they don't push themselves to *reduce the actual spending.*

Chapter One: The Five Hidden Reasons You Should Fight Back

1. The average annual cost of an American family's premiums has risen by 55 percent in the past decade, to about $21,342, according to the Kaiser Family Foundation. Deductibles—what people pay out of pocket before their benefits kick in—have climbed at the same time. The average plan doesn't pay out until each individual has paid $1,644. For families, those deductibles get multiplied. https://www.kff.org/report-section/ehbs-2020-section-1-cost-of-health-insurance/. The median monthly mortgage was $975 in 2019 in the United States, according to the American Housing Survey produced by the United States Census Bureau, https://www.census.gov/programs-surveys/ahs.html.

2. Maybe the worst part about our exorbitant health care spending is that so many people still have little or no coverage. About twenty-nine million Americans had no health insurance in 2019 and that number is rising (Health Insurance Coverage of the Total Population, Kaiser Family Foundation, accessed January 15, 2021). About 45 percent of Americans ages 19 to 64 are underinsured, meaning their out-of-pocket costs are so high they're unaffordable (Health Insurance Coverage Eight Years After the ACA, Commonwealth Fund, February 7, 2019, accessed October 7, 2019). Even more alarming: One in six Americans have medical debt in collections. For Americans of color who have medical debt collections, the number is one in five. (Debt in America: An Interactive Map, Urban Institute, 2017, accessed January 15, 2021.)

3. Ezekiel Emanuel and Victor Fuchs, "Who Really Pays for Health Care?," *Journal of the American Medical Association*, March 5, 2008.

4. Laura Snyder and Robin Rudowitz, "Medicaid Financing: How Does It Work and What Are the Implications?," Kaiser Family Foundation, KFF.org, https://www.kff.org/medicaid/issue-brief /medicaid-financing-how-does-it-work-and-what-are-the -implications/.

5. This is a line from David Contorno, a health benefits adviser I feature in chapter nine.

6. Here's a press release about the Ohio auditor's findings: "Auditor's Report: Pharmacy Benefit Managers Take Fees of 31% on Generic Drugs Worth $208M in One-Year Period," August 16, 2018, https:// ohioauditor.gov/news/pressreleases/Details/5042. The entire report is available at https://ohioauditor.gov/auditsearch/Reports/2018 /Medicaid_Pharmacy_Services_2018_Franklin.pdf.

7. The January 2021 report the investigators produced is extensive and astounding. Here's the press release: https://www.finance.senate.gov /chairmans-news/grassley-wyden-release-insulin-investigation -uncovering-business-practices-between-drug-companies-and-pbms -that-keep-prices-high, accessed January 20, 2021.

8. See page 195 of the shoppable services document on the Vassar Brothers Medical Center website: https://patients.healthquest.org /wp-content/uploads/2020/12/330023_Vassar-Brothers-Medical -Center_Consumer-Shoppable.pdf, accessed January 20, 2021.

9. See page 111 of the shoppable services document posted on the Northern Dutchess Hospital website: https://patients.healthquest .org/wp-content/uploads/2020/12/330049_Northern-Dutchess -Hospital_Consumer-Shoppable.pdf, accessed January 20, 2021.

10. Rabah Kamal et al., "How Does Health Spending in the U.S. Compare to Other Countries?," Peterson-KFF Health System Tracker: https://www.healthsystemtracker.org/chart-collection /health-spending-u-s-compare-countries/#item-spendingcomparison _health-consumption-expenditures-per-capita-2019, accessed January 15, 2021.

11. The United States spends nearly twice as much as the average developed country, but has the lowest life expectancy, highest chronic disease burden rate, and an obesity rate that's twice the average. Melinda K. Abrams and Roosa Tikkanen, "U.S. Health

Care from a Global Perspective, 2019: Higher Spending, Worse Outcomes?," Commonwealth Fund, January 30, 2020, https://www .commonwealthfund.org/publications/issue-briefs/2020/jan/us -health-care-global-perspective-2019, accessed January 16, 2021.

12. I spent a year on a quest for *ProPublica* to identify the most egregious examples of wasted health care spending in the country. Those stories are here: https://www.propublica.org/series/wasted-medicine. The project was inspired by this report: Institute of Medicine of the National Academies, *Best Care at Lower Cost: The Path to Continuously Learning Health Care in America* (Washington, D.C.: National Academies Press, 2013), https://doi.org/10.17226/13444.

13. William H. Shrank et al., "Waste in the US Health Care System," *Journal of the American Medical Association* 322, no. 15 (October 15, 2019).

14. Aliya Jiwani et al., "Billing and Insurance-Related Administrative Costs in United States Health Care: Synthesis of Micro-Costing Evidence," *BMC Health Services Research* 14, no. 556 (November 13, 2014).

15. Zirui Song and Katherine Baicker, "Effect of a Workplace Wellness Program on Employee Health and Economic Outcomes," *Journal of the American Medical Association* 321, no. 15 (April 16, 2019), https:// jamanetwork.com/journals/jama/article-abstract/2730614, accessed January 2, 2021.

16. This is a favorite line of Carl Schuessler, a health care benefits consultant in Georgia: https://www.linkedin.com/in/ccsjr1. I feature his work in chapter nine.

Chapter Two: Never Pay the First Bill

1. https://khn.org/news/tag/bill-of-the-month/.

2. The HealthCare.gov website explains the types of preventive care benefits that must be covered in more detail. Here's the link: "Preventive Care Benefits for Adults," https://www.healthcare.gov /preventive-care-adults/, accessed February 4, 2020. You can also see Section 2713 of the Patient Protection and Affordable Care Act. Or, for more detail, check out the entry in the Federal Register: "Coverage of Certain Preventive Services Under the Affordable Care

Act: A Rule by the Internal Revenue Service, the Employee Benefits Security Administration, and the Health and Human Services Department on 07/14/2015," https://www.federalregister.gov /documents/2015/07/14/2015-17076/coverage-of-certain-preventive -services-under-the-affordable-care-act, accessed February 4, 2020.

3. Calculating what Medicare pays is increasing the complexity, but it's a valuable thing to do if you think you're getting overcharged. If you show the medical provider that they are taking one amount from Medicare, it gives you leverage to negotiate a better deal if they are overcharging you. You can look up the Medicare prices for physician services here: https://www.cms.gov/apps/physician-fee-schedule/search /search-criteria.aspx. Note that the HCPCS codes for physician services are often the same as the CPT codes. Medicare has provided instructions for using the search tool: https://www.cms.gov/apps /physician-fee-schedule/help/How_to_MPFS_Booklet_ICN901344.pdf.

4. https://www.healthcare.gov/glossary/ucr-usual-customary-and -reasonable/.

5. Patient Safety Action Network Community, public Facebook group, https://www.facebook.com/groups/patientharm/, accessed February 14, 2020.

6. "4 Steps to Interview and Hire an Advocate or Care Manager," ADVOConnection Directory, https://advoconnection.com/hire-a -patient-advocate/#interview, accessed February 13, 2020.

Chapter Three: The Insurance Warrior's Guide to Winning Your Appeal

1. Laurie Todd, *Approved: Win Your Insurance Appeal in 5 Days* (Kirkland, WA: Healthwise Publications, 2018), available at http://www.theinsurancewarrior.com/books.html.

2. The problem is the laws and regulations are loaded with loopholes that work to the company's advantage.

3. Here's a link to Washington State's network adequacy law: https://apps.leg.wa.gov/wac/default.aspx?cite=284-170-200.

4. California Health and Human Services Agency, "Independent Medical Review (IMR) Determinations, Trend," CHHS Open Data, https://data.chhs.ca.gov/dataset/independent-medical-review -imr-determinations-trend, accessed March 1, 2020.

5. Todd, *Approved*, 312.

6. Marshall Allen, "How One Employer Stuck a New Mom with an $898,984 Bill for Her Premature Baby," *ProPublica*, November 4, 2019, https://www.propublica.org/article/how-one-employer-stuck-a-new -mom-with-a-bill-for-her-premature-baby, accessed March 1, 2020.

7. I've posted the masterfully researched and written appeal on my website: marshallallen.com.

Chapter Four: How to Handle Medical Debt Collectors

1. https://ripmedicaldebt.org/.

2. Be sure to cite this law when you refer to its protections in any letter you write to a debt collector. Here's a link: Fair Debt Collection Practices Act, Federal Trade Commission, https://www.ftc.gov /enforcement/rules/rulemaking-regulatory-reform-proceedings /fair-debt-collection-practices-act-text. This FAQ provides a good overview: https://www.consumer.ftc.gov/articles/debt-collection-faqs.

3. The IRS explains their policy here: "Topic No. 431 Canceled Debt—Is It Taxable or Not?," Tax Topics, https://www.irs.gov /taxtopics/tc431, accessed February 23, 2020.

4. Kenneth P. Brevoort and Michelle Kambara, "Data Point: Medical Debt and Credit Scores," Consumer Financial Protection Bureau, May 2014, https://files.consumerfinance.gov/f/201405_cfpb_report_data -point_medical-debt-credit-scores.pdf, accessed February 14, 2020.

5. www.upsolve.org.

6. Christopher Voss and Tahl Raz, *Never Split the Difference* (New York: HarperCollins, 2016).

7. William E. Bruhn et al., "Prevalence and Characteristics of Virginia Hospitals Suing Patients and Garnishing Wages for Unpaid Medical Bills," Research Letter, *Journal of the American Medical Association* 322, no. 7 (August 20, 2019): 691–92, https://jamanetwork.com /journals/jama/fullarticle/2737183.

8. https://www.restoringmedicine.org/.

9. "Adhesion Contract (Contract of Adhesion): Overview," Legal Information Institute, Cornell Law School, https://www.law.cornell .edu/wex/adhesion_contract_(contract_of_adhesion), accessed February 23, 2020.

Chapter Five: Sue Them in Small Claims Court

1. I was working on a story for *ProPublica* about the ways insurance companies use CPAP machines to monitor users and overcharge them. You can find it here: Marshall Allen, "You Snooze, You Lose: Insurers Make the Old Adage Literally True," November 21, 2018, https://www.propublica.org/article/you-snooze-you-lose-insurers -make-the-old-adage-literally-true.

2. *An Arm and a Leg* is an excellent podcast and great for anyone who wants to understand how health care *really* works and what they can do to fight back. Check out the episode where I shared Alan Levy's story here: "Whoa, This Medical Device Is Spying on Me. In My Sleep. So My Insurer Can Deny Me Coverage," season 2, episode 6, *An Arm and a Leg*, July 17, 2019, https://armandalegshow.com /episode/whoa-this-medical-device-is-spying-on-me-in-my-sleep-so -my-insurer-can-deny-me-coverage/.

3. The episode is called "Can They Freaking DO That?!?" and you can find it here: season 3, episode 5, *An Arm and a Leg*, December 12, 2019, https://armandalegshow.com/episode/can-they-freaking-do -that/. The show hit the topic again in season 4, episode 15, "A Former 'Bad Guy' Lawyer Shows Us How the Dark Machinery Works. And Our Rights," January 28, 2021, https://armandalegshow .com/episode/former-bad-guy-lawyer/.

4. "§2-305. Open Price Term," Legal Information Institute, Cornell Law School, https://www.law.cornell.edu/ucc/2/2-305.

5. The website soulsherpa.net has lots of resources for patients.

Chapter Six: How to Avoid Treatment You Don't Need

1. Judith Garber, "A Silver Lining to COVID-19: Fewer Low-Value Elective Procedures," Lown Institute, April 20, 2020, https:// lowninstitute.org/a-silver-lining-to-covid-19-fewer-low-value-elective -procedures/.

2. "Final Recommendation Statement: Cervical Cancer: Screening," U.S. Preventive Services Task Force, August 21, 2018, https://www .uspreventiveservicestaskforce.org/uspstf/recommendation/cervical -cancer-screening; and "American College of Physicians Releases Best Practice Advice for the Proper Time, Test, and Interval for

Cervical Cancer Screening," ACP Newsroom, American College of Physicians, April 30, 2015, https://www.acponline.org/acp-newsroom /american-college-of-physicians-releases-best-practice-advice-for-the -proper-time-test-and-interval.

3. "Lab Tests Before Surgery: When You Need Them—and When You Don't," ChoosingWisely.org, n.d., https://www.choosingwisely.org /patient-resources/lab-tests-before-surgery/, accessed November 20, 2020.

4. Howard LeWine, M.D., "Physical Therapy as Good as Surgery and Less Risky for One Type of Lower Back Pain," Harvard Health Publishing, Harvard Medical School, April 9, 2015, https://www .health.harvard.edu/blog/physical-therapy-as-good-as-surgery-and -less-risky-for-one-type-of-lower-back-pain-201504097863.

5. "First, Do No Harm. Calculating Health Care Waste in Washington State," Washington Health Alliance, February 2018, https://www .wacommunitycheckup.org/media/47156/2018-first-do-no-harm.pdf, accessed January 29, 2021.

6. James S. Yeh et al., "Association of Industry Payments to Physicians with the Prescribing of Brand-Name Statins in Massachusetts," *JAMA Internal Medicine* (May 2016), https://jamanetwork.com /journals/jamainternalmedicine/fullarticle/2520680, accessed January 28, 2021.

7. Laurence C. Baker, "Acquisition of MRI Equipment by Doctors Drives Up Imaging Use and Spending," *Health Affairs* 29, no. 12 (December 2010), https://pubmed.ncbi.nlm.nih.gov/21134927/.

8. Vikas Saini et al., "Drivers of Poor Medical Care," *Lancet* 390, no. 10090 (July 8, 2017): 178–90, https://www.thelancet.com/journals /lancet/article/PIIS0140-6736(16)30947-3/fulltext.

9. You can see the full story I wrote for *ProPublica* here: Marshall Allen, "A Hospital Charged $1,877 to Pierce a 5-Year-Old's Ears. This Is Why Health Care Costs So Much," November 28, 2017, https:// www.propublica.org/article/a-hospital-charged-to-pierce-ears-why -health-care-costs-so-much.

10. Kao-Ping Chua et al., "Differences in the Receipt of Low-Value Services Between Publicly and Privately Insured Children," *Pediatrics* 145, no. 2 (January 2020), https://pediatrics

.aappublications.org/content/early/2020/01/03/peds.2019
-2325?versioned=true.

11. Mei-Sing Ong and Kenneth Mandl, "National Expenditure for
False-Positive Mammograms and Breast Cancer Overdiagnoses
Estimated at $4 Billion a Year," *Health Affairs* 34, no. 4 (April 2015),
https://www.healthaffairs.org/doi/full/10.1377/hlthaff.2014.1087.

12. Arenas offered to waive her privacy rights so the practice that
provided her treatment could speak to me. Officials from the
practice declined to talk to me about it. Her medical records show
that in response to reviews by her insurance company and the
attorney general's office, her doctors said the care was appropriate.

13. Learn about the task force and see its recommendations here: https://
www.uspreventiveservicestaskforce.org/.

14. See "Conflict of Interest Disclosures," U.S. Preventive Services Task
Force, https://www.uspreventiveservicestaskforce.org/Page/Name
/conflict-of-interest-disclosures.

15. The guidelines are updated periodically as the task force continues to
review emerging research, https://www.uspreventiveservicestaskforce
.org/uspstf/recommendation/breast-cancer-screening.

16. The Centers for Disease Control and Prevention has a summary
here: https://www.cdc.gov/cancer/breast/pdf/breast-cancer-screening
-guidelines-508.pdf.

17. Cathryn Jakobson Ramin's book *Crooked* (New York: Harper, 2018)
is an excellent resource if you are considering spinal surgery.

18. LeWine, "Physical Therapy as Good as Surgery."

19. Martin A. Makary and Michael Daniel, "Medical Error—the Third
Leading Cause of Death in the U.S.," *BMJ*, May 2016, https://www
.bmj.com/content/353/bmj.i2139, accessed January 16, 2021.

20. "5 Questions to Ask Your Doctor Before You Get Any Test,
Treatment, or Procedure," ChoosingWisely.org, https://www
.choosingwisely.org/wp-content/uploads/2018/03/5-Questions
-Poster_8.5x11-Eng.pdf, accessed January 29, 2021.

Chapter Seven: Protect Yourself from Price Gouging

1. A shout-out to the folks at NBC who used the "No Pay, No Spray"
headline in a story they ran on October 5, 2020, about an *actual*

for-profit fire department, http://www.nbcnews.com/id/39516346/ns
/us_news-life/t/no-pay-no-spray-firefighters-let-home-burn/#.Xf
-NBodKiUk.

2. Bricker now makes awesome explainer videos that help people
   understand how the medical industry actually works. Check them
   out at AHealthcareZ.com.

3. Bricker pointed out that our society also has inelastic demand for
   things like electricity, or water, or phone services and broadband
   internet. We are not expected to go without them. But in those cases
   the government regulates the private companies that provide our
   households and companies with these needs, allowing them to
   receive a fixed return on their investment. They're not allowed to
   charge whatever they want or jack up prices beyond what people can
   afford. If regulators didn't put some cost controls in place the entire
   population could be exploited. We'd be paying way more than we do
   now for electricity and water—because we can't control our demand.

4. Elisabeth Rosenthal, MD, "When High Prices Mean Needless
   Death," *JAMA Internal Medicine* 179, no. 1 (January 2019): 114–15,
   https://jamanetwork.com/journals/jamainternalmedicine/fullarticle
   /2717498.

5. Rosenthal, "When High Prices Mean Needless Death."

6. The gaming of insulin prices is laid out in stark detail in a
   report by the Senate Finance Committee: https://www.finance
   .senate.gov/imo/media/doc/Grassley-Wyden%20Insulin%20
   Report%20(FINAL%201).pdf.

7. Quizzify is a heath care literacy company that uses entertaining
   quizzes and other techniques to cut through and debunk a lot of the
   nonsense in the medical industry. You can sign up for their email
   free and they also have paid products for employers to help their
   employees. Check them out at quizzify.com.

8. The medical industry calls it cost shifting when it makes people
   covered by employer-sponsored health plans pay more than what the
   government health plans pay. It's been going on for decades and isn't
   even a secret in the industry. The industry's justification for making
   working Americans pay extra for the same thing is that it must make
   up for the alleged losses being suffered because of the uninsured

patients, or patients covered by Medicare and Medicaid, which pay less than the commercial plans. I say "alleged" losses because Medicare rates are set based on what experts consider a fair price to cover the medical provider's costs. Also, hospitals could reduce the amount of money they're wasting on things like building campaigns and layers of administrators who get paid massive executive salaries. They could lower their costs. But those facts don't get into the justifications the industry uses to discriminate against patients on commercial insurance plans. A couple of years ago I sat in the fancy office of a hospital chief executive and asked her and the facility's chief financial officer where the idea of cost shifting even came from. They said it's been going on for decades, as long as they'd been in the industry. The CEO said it may go back to the 1980s, when Medicare began paying a flat rate based on the type of service a hospital provided. Since the Medicare rates are set, the hospitals can bring in more money from the commercial insurance companies—which negotiate on behalf of themselves and the self-funded employers whose plans they administer. "I think we've been cost shifting for a very long time," the CFO told me. I had to ask the hospital executives how it can be considered fair to make patients in employer-sponsored health plans pay more than what government plans pay. Isn't cost shifting unfair? I asked them. "It's unfortunate the way it's set up," the CFO conceded.

9. Chapin White, "Hospital Prices in Indiana. Findings from an Employer-Led Transparency Initiative," RAND Corporation, 2017, https://www.rand.org/pubs/research_reports/RR2106.html, accessed September 17, 2020.

10. Christopher M. Whaley et al., "Nationwide Evaluation of Health Care Prices Paid by Private Health Plans," RAND Corporation, 2020, https://www.rand.org/pubs/research_reports/RR4394.html, accessed October 1, 2020.

11. The Medicare Procedure Price Lookup Comparison File is available here: https://www.cms.gov/license/ama?file=/files/zip/procedure -price-lookup-comparison-file-2020.zip.

12. https://www.medicare.gov/procedure-price-lookup/.

13. Tanaka, Miho J., MD, "Ambulatory Surgery Centers Versus Hospital-based Outpatient Departments: What's the Difference?"

AAOS Now. September 1, 2019. https://www.aaos.org/aaosnow/2019
/sep/managing/managing02.

14. Jayne O'Donnell and Shari Rudavsky, "Need an MRI? It Pays to
Shop Around. Big Time." USA Today Network. March 28, 2017.
https://www.usatoday.com/story/news/politics/2017/03/28/mri-costs
-vary-widely-same-areas-but-hospitals-usually-priciest/99685534/.

15. "We found wide variation in the prices health insurance companies
pay providers for similar services, unexplained by differences in
quality, complexity of services, or other common measures of
consumer value." That's how they put it on page 1 of the
Massachusetts attorney general's 2015 "Examination of Health Care
Cost Trends and Cost Drivers," https://archives.lib.state.ma.us
/bitstream/handle/2452/266242/ocn748592595-2015-09-18.pdf,
accessed January 28, 2021.

16. "Quality indicators for high-price hospitals were mixed: High-
price hospitals fared much better than low-price hospitals did in
U.S. News & World Report rankings, which are largely based on
reputation, while generally scoring worse on objective measures
of quality, such as postsurgical mortality rates." Chapin White
et al., "Understanding Differences Between High- and Low-Price
Hospitals: Implications for Efforts to Rein in Costs," *Health Affairs*
33, no. 2 (February 2014): 324–31, https://www.healthaffairs.org/doi
/pdf/10.1377/hlthaff.2013.0747/.

17. https://nationalhealthcouncil.org/blog/blog-president-trumps
-executive-order-pricing-transparency/.

18. https://www.jdpower.com/sites/default/files/file/2020-05/2020053
%20U.S.%20Commercial%20Member%20Health%20Plan.pdf.

Chapter Eight: You Might Save Money by *Not* Using Your Insurance

1. Robin A. Cohen and Emily P. Zammitti, "High-Deductible Health
Plan Enrollment Among Adults Aged 18–64 with Employment-
Based Insurance Coverage," Centers for Disease Control, NCHS
Data Brief No. 317, August 2018, https://www.cdc.gov/nchs/products
/databriefs/db317.htm, accessed January 22, 2020.

2. Karen Van Nuys et al., "Overpaying for Prescription Drugs: The
Copay Clawback Phenomenon," Leonard D. Schaeffer Center for

Health Policy & Economics, University of Southern California, https://healthpolicy.usc.edu/wp-content/uploads/2018/03/2018.03 _Overpaying%20for%20Prescription%20Drugs_White%20Paper_v.1-2.pdf.

3. Daniel Arnold and Christopher Whaley, "Who Pays for Health Care Costs?," RAND Corporation, July 2020, https://www.rand.org /pubs/working_papers/WRA621-2.html.

4. https://www.propublica.org/article/why-your-health-insurer-does -not-care-about-your-big-bills.

5. Andy Sher, "Health Care Data Firm Defends Report on Medical Overcharges Paid by Tennessee Insurance Plan Administrators to Providers," *Chattanooga Times Free Press*, October 16, 2020, https://www.timesfreepress.com/news/local/story/2020/oct/16 /data-firm-defends-report/534254/.

6. "Infographic—US Health Care Spending: Who Pays?," California Health Care Foundation, May 22, 2019. https://www.chcf.org /publication/us-health-care-spending-who-pays/, accessed January 24, 2020.

7. They can be found at GoodRx.com.

8. Charles Ornstein and Katie Thomas, "When Buying Prescription Drugs, Some Pay More with Insurance Than Without It," *ProPublica* and *New York Times*, December 9, 2017, https://www .propublica.org/article/when-buying-prescription-drugs-some-pay -more-with-insurance-than-without-it. The reporters also put together a guide that explains "How to Save Money on Your Prescription Drugs," available at https://www.propublica.org/article /how-to-save-money-on-your-prescription-drugs.

9. Van Nuys et al., "Overpaying for Prescription Drugs."

Part III: Employer Section

1. I love how the author Maria Konnikova describes a confidence artist in her book *The Confidence Game*, because it could just as easily apply to the medical industry's exploitation of American employers: "Their genius," she says of the con artist, "lies in figuring out what, precisely, it is we want, and how they can present themselves as the perfect vehicle for delivering on that desire. . . . The true con artist doesn't force us to do anything; he makes us complicit in our

own undoing. He doesn't steal. We give. He doesn't have to threaten us. We supply the story ourselves. We believe because we want to, not because anyone made us." Maria Konnikova, *The Confidence Game: Why We Fall for It . . . Every Time* (New York: Penguin Books, 2016), 5–6.

Chapter Nine: The Conflict of Interest Undermining Employers' Purchase of Health Benefits

1. https://www.propublica.org/article/lavish-bonus-luxury-trip-health -benefits-brokers-will-have-to-disclose-what-they-receive-from-the -insurance-industry.

2. Panle Jia Barwick, Parag A. Pathak, and Masie Wong, "Conflicts of Interest and Steering in Residential Brokerage," *American Economic Journal: Applied Economics* 9, no. 3 (July 2017): 191–222, https://www .aeaweb.org/articles?id=10.1257/app.20160214.

3. Jeremy Burke et al., "Impacts of Conflicts of Interest in the Financial Services Industry," RAND Labor & Population Working Paper, February 2015, https://www.rand.org/content/dam/rand/pubs /working_papers/WR1000/WR1076/RAND_WR1076.pdf.

4. "Regulation Best Interest: A Small Entity Compliance Guide," Securities and Exchange Commission, https://www.sec.gov/info /smallbus/secg/regulation-best-interest.

5. Hannah Fresques, "Doctors Prescribe More of a Drug If They Receive Money from a Pharma Company Tied to It," *ProPublica*, December. 20, 2019, https://www.propublica.org/article/doctors -prescribe-more-of-a-drug-if-they-receive-money-from-a-pharma -company-tied-to-it.

6. Manvi Sharma et al., "Association Between Industry Payments and Prescribing Costly Medications: An Observational Study Using Open Payments and Medicare Part D Data," *BMC Health Services Research* 18, no. 236 (April 2, 2018), https://bmchealthservres .biomedcentral.com/articles/10.1186/s12913-018-3043-8.

7. Ge Bai et al., "The Commissions Paid to Brokers for Fully-Insured Health Plans," Johns Hopkins Carey Business School, November 2020, https://journals.sagepub.com/doi/abs/10.1177/107755 8720980561.

8. Wincline did an analysis of the exorbitant TPA fees that you can find here: https://wincline.com/tpa-hidden-revenue/.

9. Schuessler recommends that every employer ask their insurance provider how much of their premium is being spent on claims. In some states it's required by law, he said. The Georgia law requires that insurers furnish claims experience within the thirty days of the policyholder's request: https://law.justia.com/codes/georgia/2017/title-33/chapter-30/article-1/section-33-30-13.1/, accessed January 16, 2021.

10. HRI Benefits Advisor Compensation Disclosure Form, Health Rosetta, https://healthrosetta.org/learn/benefits-advisor-disclosure/.

Chapter Ten: The Buyer Sets the Price

1. I loved writing about Bartlett for *ProPublica* because her story is so prescriptive, and even the hurdles she had to overcome show that success is possible. Here's the original story: https://www.propublica.org/article/in-montana-a-tough-negotiator-proved-employers-do-not-have-to-pay-so-much-for-health-care.

2. Michael A. Morrisey, *Health Insurance*, 2nd ed. (Chicago: Health Administration Press, 2020). This book has been a huge help to me as I learn about the health insurance industry.

3. https://www.rand.org/pubs/research_reports/RR4394.html.

4. I have heard from some sources that this fiduciary duty may make employers more at risk than they realize for the way they manage their health plans. Employers are legally required to run the plan prudently, in the sole interest of the participants and beneficiaries—the workers. Some say class-action lawsuits may be on the horizon for employers who fail to fulfill this fiduciary role. Here's more about the fiduciary role: https://www.dol.gov/general/topic/health-plans/fiduciaryresp.

5. Amanda Schiavo, "Steel Company Saves $5M on Health Benefits Through Reference-Based Pricing," *Employee Benefit News*, July 9, 2019, https://www.benefitnews.com/news/pacific-steel-finds-ways-to-save-on-healthcare, accessed January 7, 2021.

6. "Auditor's Report: Pharmacy Benefit Managers Take Fees of 31% on Generic Drugs Worth $208M in One-Year Period," August 16, 2018,

https://ohioauditor.gov/news/pressreleases/Details/5042. The entire report is available at https://ohioauditor.gov/auditsearch/Reports /2018/Medicaid_Pharmacy_Services_2018_Franklin.pdf.

7. "Medicaid Pharmacy Pricing: Opening the Black Box," Kentucky Cabinet for Health and Family Service, Office of Health Data Analytics, Department for Medicaid Services, February 19, 2019, https://chfs.ky.gov/agencies/ohda/Documents1/CHFSMedicaid PharmacyPricing.pdf.

8. 3 Axis Advisors, "Analysis of PBM Spread Pricing in Michigan Medicaid Managed Care," April 28, 2019, https://static1.squarespace .com/static/5c326d5596e76f58ee234632/t/5cc5eb7b24a6944974537e28 /1556474768436/3AA+MI+Medicaid+managed+care+analysis +-+Final+04.10.19.pdf. Here's the press release from the Michigan Pharmacists Association: https://www.michiganpharmacists.org /news/ID/2532/New-Report-Highlights-Role-of-Pharmacy-Benefit -Managers-in-Manipulating-Drug-Costs-for-Michigan-Patients -Pharmacists-and-Taxpayers.

9. 3 Axis Advisors, "Analysis of PBM Spread Pricing in New York Medicaid Managed Care," Pharmacists Society of the State of New York, January 17, 2019, http://www.ncpa.co/pdf/state-advoc /new-york-report.pdf. The Pharmacists Society of the State of New York put out a press release: https://cdn.ymaws.com/pssny .site-ym .com/resource/resmgr/press/FixRx_Study_news _release.pdf.

10. Marilyn Bartlett, Maureen Hensley-Quinn, and Trish Riley, "NASHP's New Hospital Cost Tool Informs State Cost-Containment Strategies," September 28, 2020, https://www.nashp .org/nashps-new-hospital-cost-tool-informs-state-cost-containment -strategies/.

11. "High Health Status," America's Health Rankings, 2020, https:// www.americashealthrankings.org/explore/annual/measure/Health _Status/state/CO.

12. "The Colorado Purchasing Alliance," Colorado Business Group on Health, https://cbghealth.org/the-colorado-purchasing-alliance/.

13. Whaley, "Nationwide Evaluation of Health Care Prices."

Chapter Eleven: Check Your Receipts. You Might Be a Victim of Fraud.

1. It resulted in this story: Marshall Allen, "A Doctor Went to His Own Employer for a COVID-19 Antibody Test. It Cost $10,984," September 5, 2020, https://www.propublica.org/article/a-doctor -went-to-his-own-employer-for-a-covid-19-antibody-test-it-cost -10-984.

2. "National Health Expenditures 2019 Highlights," Centers for Medicare and Medicaid Services, https://www.cms.gov/files /document/highlights.pdf.

3. For more about this unbelievable scam, check out my story for *ProPublica:* Marshall Allen, "Health Insurers Make It Easy for Scammers to Steal Millions. Who Pays? You," July 19, 2019, https://www.propublica.org/article/health-insurers-make-it-easy -for-scammers-to-steal-millions-who-pays-you.

4. You can find them at ClaimInformatics.com. Scott Haas, a consultant who works for USI Insurance Services: https:// healthrosetta.org/people/scott-haas.

5. See the original story I wrote for *ProPublica* for all the details about my inquiries. You can find it here: Marshall Allen, "We Asked Prosecutors If Health Insurance Companies Care About Fraud. They Laughed at Us," September 10, 2019, https://www.propublica.org /article/we-asked-prosecutors-if-health-insurance-companies-care -about-fraud-they-laughed-at-us.

6. Marshall Allen, "What Happens When a Health Plan Has No Limits? An Acupuncturist Earns $677 a Session," *ProPublica*, December 19, 2019, https://www.propublica.org/article/what -happens-when-a-health-plan-for-teachers-has-no-limits-an -acupuncturist-earns-677-a-session.

Index

About the Author

MARSHALL ALLEN is a reporter for *ProPublica*, where he investigates both patient safety and why we pay so much for health care and get so little in return. He is a Pulitzer Prize finalist and recipient of the Harvard Kennedy School's Goldsmith Prize for Investigative Reporting. He teaches investigative reporting at the Craig Newmark Graduate School of Journalism at the City University of New York and has spoken at various conferences across the country. Before he became a journalist, Marshall spent five years in full-time ministry, including three years in Kenya.

Never Pay the First Bill is Marshall's first book. Writing it led him to launch Allen Health Academy to further his efforts to empower consumers with a series of health literacy videos. For more information, and to sign up for his newsletter or contact him, go to marshallallen.com. He loves to hear about consumers who take on the system and enjoys sharing winning tactics with the public—so please reach out!

Marshall lives in Fanwood, New Jersey, with his wife, Sonja, and their three boys, Isaac, Ashton, and Cody.